TEACHING ORAL COMMUNICATION

Applied Language Studies
Edited by David Crystal and Keith Johnson

This new series aims to deal with key topics within the main branches of applied language studies – initially in the fields of foreign language teaching and learning, child language acquisition and clinical or remedial language studies. The series will provide students with a research perspective in a particular topic, at the same time containing an original slant which will make each volume a genuine contribution to the development of ideas in the subject.

Series List

TEACHING ORAL COMMUNICATION

A METHODOLOGICAL FRAMEWORK

William Littlewood

BLACKWELL
Oxford UK & Cambridge USA

First published 1992

Blackwell Publishers
108 Cowley Road
Oxford OX4 1JF
UK

Three Cambridge Center
Cambridge, Massachusetts 02142
USA

British Library Cataloguing in Publication Data
A CIP catalogue record for this book is available from the British Library.

Library of Congress Cataloging-in-Publication Data

Littlewood, William.
    Teaching oral communications : a methodological framework /
William Littlewood.
        p.   cm. — (applied language studies)
    Includes bibliographical references and index.
    ISBN 0–631–15455–8 (alk. paper). — ISBN 0–631–15456–6 (pbk. :
alk. paper)
        1. Language and languages—Study and teaching. 2. Oral
communication—Study and teaching.   I. Title.   II. Series.
P53.6.L57   1992   91–43821
302.2′242′07—dc20   CIP

Phototypeset in 11 on 13pt Ehrhardt
by Intype, London
Printed in Great Britain by Biddles Ltd, Guildford

This book is printed on acid-free paper.

Contents

Introduction

Practice, Principles and Methodology

Nowadays teachers have access to an immense repertoire of materials and activities for teaching a foreign language. In addition to the range that any modern course-book contains, many more are to be found in the rich stock of language-teaching handbooks and magazines that are now available. Indeed, at a materials development workshop that I organized recently, some teachers perceived their problem as being not primarily how to *develop* activities and materials at all, but how to *select* from the multitude that were already available to them. Of course, many teachers will continue to see the creative process of developing unique materials as an essential part of their profession, but what these particular teachers' views indicate is that nobody's repertoire needs now to be lacking in interesting and exciting activities.

However, it is not sufficient to have access to a wide range of activities. A teacher can know a thousand or more interesting activities; they are of limited use in the classroom unless he or she also possesses a framework of principles for selecting appropriate activities for particular learning purposes. This framework must answer questions about the fundamental nature of these activities, such as:

- How does the activity in which the learners engage relate to their communicative goals?
- What kinds of learning processes is the activity most likely to activate?
- How does the learning that takes place contribute to the overall process of learning to communicate?

- How does the activity relate to other activities which share similar characteristics?
- What role should the teacher try to adopt and what roles should be assigned to the learners?

A framework of principles which answer questions such as these, combined with a repertoire of activities for translating them into classroom practice, is what I here mean by the term 'methodology'. It is neither pure theory, nor pure practice, but links the two. It is a kind of conceptual map of classroom reality which both integrates ideas from various sources and orients the teacher to particular kinds of action.

Many important developments in language teaching in the past fifty years have been stimulated by the search for the 'right method', which would provide ready solutions to all our language-teaching problems. It was in this spirit that, for example, the audio-lingual method and the audio-visual method were advocated in numerous parts of the world in the 1950s and 1960s. The search proved inconclusive and we have now come to realize that no single pre-scribed set of procedures can be valid for all learners, all situations and all teachers. We are therefore now more inclined to base our teaching on a looser framework of principles and practices which provide guidance and direction but allow individual teachers to shape their classroom approach in ways appropriate to their own circum-stances.

In the end, then, every teacher designs his or her own methodology by creating a unique combination of insights, preferences and proce-dures. However, if this combination is to be as effective as possible, it cannot be purely arbitrary: it must be based on the best available knowledge about the nature of language and learning as well as the best available experience of other teachers pursuing similar goals. On the basis of this knowledge and experience, we can seek to develop a methodological framework which is (a) composed of a coherent and justifiable body of ideas and (b) capable of producing purposeful and effective action in the classroom. At the same time it can be sufficiently flexible for teachers to adapt it to their own situations and amend it in the light of their own experience.

The Present Book

The purpose of the present book mirrors the term 'methodology' in the sense that I have used it above: it is neither purely theoretical nor purely practical but aims to link the two. It is about the 'map of classroom reality' which guides our actions in the classroom.

One important element that makes up this map is our set of beliefs about language itself and how it serves communication. This is the topic of Part I of the book. Chapter 1 looks at how language serves communication and how the grammar provides us with a system of signals for conveying meanings. Chapter 2 examines the *kinds* of meaning that language can express and how it enables people to engage in social interaction. It relates the discussion to the different goals that people have when they set about learning to use a foreign language.

The second most important element in the map is our set of beliefs about learning. This is the topic of Part II of the book. Chapter 3 views language learning as a process of skill-learning. This is probably the view that has been dominant in the classrooms that most of us have known, either as teachers or as learners. Chapter 4 views language learning as a process of natural growth – a view that has become widespread recently as people have looked at first-language learning and second-language learning in natural settings. Neither view is 'wrong' and so chapter 5 asks how they might be integrated into a single framework which can provide a basis for our methodology.

It is to this methodology that Part III turns. Building on the perspectives on language presented in Part I and the perspectives on learning presented in Part II, chapter 6 suggests a framework which links the various types of activities at our disposal to each other and to the goals of language learning. Chapter 7 adopts a more global perspective on the classroom and looks at the different means that we have at our disposal for involving the learners in what we offer them.

This book does not provide detailed lists or descriptions of specific learning activities. The classroom activities that are mentioned are intended to provide illustrations of activity-types rather than to extend the reader's repertoire of practical techniques. As I said at the outset, there is now a large number of books which describe specific learning activities, and in chapters 6 and 7, I have ensured that there are references to a comprehensive selection of them. What the present book aims to do is to clarify and extend the conceptual framework from which these activities derive their justification and purpose.

As the title indicates, my main orientation in the book is towards oral communication skills. This is mainly because a limit had to be drawn somewhere and I felt that, if I had included writing, the book would have become unwieldy and lost its focus. However, much of the discussion in Parts I and II could be transferred directly to the written word. The framework presented in Part III, too, can easily be extended to accommodate writing activities.

In writing the book I have tried to keep a particular kind of reader in mind. I have tried to write for the teacher whose school authorities have decided to introduce a so-called 'communicative curriculum' but who has not had the opportunity to contribute to the discussions (theoretical and practical) which have led to this decision. This is a common situation in many countries that I know. It often means that the individual teacher is simply presented with lists of syllabus items classified in communicative terms ('topics', 'functions' etc.) but given little guidance as to the rationale that has led people to organize the syllabus in this way. In such a situation it is only natural that many teachers try to transplant the new syllabus into a teaching approach which is contrary to the principles that created the syllabus in the first place. At one extreme this can lead to functional language being translated and analysed according to traditional 'grammar-translation' procedures. More often, it can lead to the language for expressing different functions being drilled and memorized as separate items, without ever really becoming part of a creative system for communicating new meanings. Indeed sometimes the nature of public examinations is a positive encouragement to this approach: in some examining systems, learners who memorize the responses required by a predictable range of personal questions or role-playing tasks may be assured of at least a reasonable end-result.

My hope is that the material in the book will help such readers to orient themselves more happily within the communicative curriculum and to develop in their students a more satisfying level of communicative ability.

Part I Language

Introduction

Richards and Rodgers (1986) analyse teaching methods by means of a framework that has three levels:

1 In the classroom itself the teacher employs *procedures*, which Richards and Rodgers describe as 'the actual moment-to-moment techniques, practices and behaviours that operate in teaching a language'.

2 Classroom procedures are selected in the light of decisions that have been made prior to the classroom, at the level of *design*: the level at which teachers (or other parties such as education authorities) decide such matters as objectives, course organization, suitable activity-types, and the roles of learners, teachers and materials.

3 In their turn, these matters of design are determined by the teacher's *approach*: 'theories about the nature of language and learning that serve as the source of practices and principles in language teaching'.

To take an example: a theory of language that emphasizes (at the level of 'approach') the separate structures of the system is likely to lead us (at the level of 'design') to describe our objectives in terms of grammatical structures and devise activity-types which enable the learners to internalize them (drills etc.). In the classroom (at the level of 'procedure') we might organize sequences of specific drills and other activities, correct any structural errors the students make, and so on.

The two chapters in Part I of this book are at the level of 'approach'. They are about the *theory of language* that underpins the communicative curriculum.

In chapter 1 I begin with the notion of 'communication', which is the aim of almost all language courses nowadays, and discuss the ways in which language functions in it. An important theme is that communication is served by signals provided by the grammatical and lexical system and that, depending on the level of communication that students wish to participate in, they need to develop adequate levels of ability to use this system creatively.

In chapter 2 the focus moves to the ways in which language enables people to interact with each other. First it looks at the kinds of meanings that language enables us to exchange. Then it examines how a conversation is created by the participants and how important aspects such as turn-taking are 'managed' through linguistic as well as non-linguistic signals.

In other words, language is seen as a structural system but one whose primary function is to enable communication to take place. It is this view of language that underpins the communicative curriculum.

1 Using Language for Communication

1.1 Introduction

Communication and language are very closely related but they are not the same phenomenon.

On the one hand, language does not only enable us to communicate with other people. It also has important mental functions and affects how we understand and reflect on the world around us. Our experience of language in social settings leads us to categorize the world in similar ways to people around us and to manipulate these categories in our thinking (see Bruner and Haste, 1987; Halliday, 1987; Vygotsky, 1962). We must not underestimate the importance of this cognitive aspect for foreign-language learners, whose encounter with a new language requires them to cope with new categories of experience and new ways of manipulating them.

Nor, on the other hand, is language the only means by which we communicate. In a noisy situation, for example, we often resort to gestures to convey simple messages; amongst people who know each other well, an ironical facial expression can be so powerful that it can completely reverse the superficial meaning of the words it accompanies (Argyle, 1978); and in everyday conversation, non-verbal signals such as posture and eye-contact play an important part in regulating turn-taking between speakers (see Beattie, 1983).

However, even though language and communication exist separately, they are obviously linked to each other in inextricable ways. It is the urge to communicate that stimulates language to grow in children (cf. Bruner, 1975; Halliday, 1975), and for adults, too, the most important function of language is to facilitate communication with others. Conversely, as we shall see later in this chapter, from the moment communication moves beyond the 'here-and-now', it relies for its success on the resources that the language system puts at its disposal.

Today most foreign-language teaching is oriented towards the development of communication skills. I therefore propose to take the notion of 'communication' rather than 'language' as the starting point for this chapter and ask first what we can learn about communication from situations where no language is used at all. This will quickly take us to situations where language is used and help us to consider what role this language performs.

1.2   Communication without Language

Here is a simple example of communication without language:

> We are in a junior-school classroom. The children are all talking together in groups, trying to solve a maths problem. The teacher now wants them to stop talking and report their conclusions. She claps her hands. The children stop their discussions.

The teacher speaks no words and yet she effectively communicates to the children that they should now 'stop talking.' How is this possible?

(1)   The first condition is, obviously, that the class can actually hear the sound of clapping and distinguish it from other sounds in the environment, such as moving chairs and banging desks. In other words they must be able to identify and process the particular *medium* (sound) that the teacher chooses to carry her message, and the specific *signal* that she transmits through that medium.

Similarly, with a foreign language, the first requirement is that the learner must identify and process foreign sounds which often seem at first like unstructured noise.

(2)   The second condition is that, by some convention established between the teacher and the class, this signal must be linked with the notion of 'stopping talking'. The link between clapping and this

particular meaning is not a necessary part of the nature of the world: it depends on the teacher and the class sharing the same *code* for converting signals to meanings.

Foreign-language learning, too, involves gaining access to a new conventional code for converting signals to meanings. But of course this soon involves much more than just linking single signals to single meanings: both the signal-system itself (the foreign language) and the network of meanings to be conveyed have their own complex structure.

(3)   Next day we see the teacher clap her hands again, but this time the signal has a completely different effect. The children are standing on a stage ready to act out a small play. When they hear the signal, they do not *stop* talking but *start*, as they begin to act their play.

What this new episode makes clear is that the conventional meaning of hand-clapping is not simply 'stop talking.' Nor, on the other hand, is it simply 'start your play.' It is something more general, such as 'now do whatever you know you are required to do in the present situation.' It is only by taking this 'present situation' into account and knowing 'what they are required to do' in it that the children can interpret the specific meaning that the teacher wants to convey on that particular occasion.

Similarly, in learning to communicate in a foreign language, it will never be enough to learn a set list of 'signals' (whether these be words, phrases or structures) and a corresponding list of 'meanings'. In order to express and understand specific messages, learners will need to relate the signals to the whole situation where communication takes place.

This brief look at non-verbal communication has enabled us to see in simplified form some important aspects of communication and some of the skills it involves. Presenting these from the point of view of foreign-language learners: the foreign language will be a new *signal-system* that they must learn to process; they will need to learn a new *code* for connecting the signals with the range of meanings that has been established by convention; and they will have to develop the ability to process the language on particular occasions, where their background knowledge (e.g. of the situation and the world) will enable them to narrow down the range of *possible* meanings and perceive the *specific* meaning appropriate to the situation.

1.3   Communication through Language

We can now see what difference it makes to communication when we begin to exploit the resources of the language system.

1.3.1   Communication with fixed items

In its simplest form, communication with language can be very similar to the non-verbal communication just described. Let us imagine that, next time the teacher needs to stop the children's discussions, she does not clap her hands but calls out 'Right!' or 'OK!'. This signal is not much more complex than clapping. However, it is drawn from the most important code that the teacher and the children share: their common language.

A lot of language use is of this simple kind. For example:

> A woman goes into a room, looks at some pictures on the wall and exclaims to her friend: 'Beautiful!'.
>
> A man goes into an information office, enquires when the next bus leaves for Swansea, comes out and says to his friend: 'Tomorrow'.

In each case the speaker and the hearer share such a lot of back-ground knowledge and the message is so simple – a single response, a single piece of information – that one word is enough to convey the message with perfect clarity.

There are many situations in which people communicate with single words not because this is most effective but because they have not yet learnt enough language to communicate in any other way. The most familiar situation is that of the infant learning a first language (cf. Crystal, 1986; de Villiers and de Villiers, 1979). In the early stages, a single word often carries the weight of meaning that would be expressed by an adult in a full utterance, and it is only by relating the word to the concrete situation that we can interpret the child's meaning. Thus on different occasions the cry 'teddy!' might be an expression of joy that teddy has come, a request for someone to fetch teddy, a lament that teddy has been taken away or a comment that teddy is present. A foreigner trying to communicate in an unknown language might use single words in a similar way. I recall here my own first visit to Spain, when I knew no Spanish except for isolated words that I could look up in a dictionary. By using these words in combination with gestures and the concrete situation (sometimes, too, in simple juxtaposition with each other), I was able to communicate enough simple messages to satisfy my basic survival needs. Immigrants are often obliged to use language in a similar way when they arrive in their new home country (cf. Cook, 1991; Ellis, 1985; Hatch, 1978; Littlewood, 1984; McLaughlin, 1987).

The fixed items that make up this simple kind of communication can be not only words but also whole phrases. Many visitors to a new country make an early point of learning a few greetings and other social rituals ('Good morning!', 'Nice to meet you') without knowing anything about how the language works. From there it is only a small step to learning phrases in which one slot can be filled with a range of alternatives in order to carry out simple transactions: 'Can I have a (sandwich/coffee/ice-cream etc.), please.' Again, routine patterns like these are often found in the early repertoire of new immigrants.

1.3.2   Communicating through the language system

What new possibilities open up when a speaker begins to use the grammatical system of the language? We can begin to answer that question by returning to an earlier example and extending it.

> A woman enters a room, sees some pictures on the wall and exclaims 'Beautiful!' to her friend.

(1)   As it stands, the communication depends on the hearer associating the word 'beautiful' with a particular concept and relating it to the physical presence of the pictures. It does not depend on any knowledge of the grammatical system of the language.

(2)   Let us now imagine that as well as the pictures there are some marble statues in the room. The woman now needs to distinguish what (or who) in the situation she is calling 'beautiful'. If she knew nothing of English grammar she might still be able to point. She might even simply juxtapose two words: 'picture – beautiful!'. How-

ever, if pointing is not clear enough and she wants to use acceptable English, she now has to use the grammatical system in order to construct a sentence: 'The pictures are beautiful.'

Note that the grammar of the language has made her go beyond the purely functional demands of the situation and signal three additional facts which the hearer already knows: the article *the* signals that she is talking about specific pictures which are familiar to the hearer; the ending *s* (on 'pictures') signals that there are two or more of them; and the verb *are* signals that they are present at this moment.

(3)   Although these additional grammatical signals add no new information in the situation just described, they introduce an important new dimension into communication: the meanings which they express are now embodied *in the language itself* and exist independently of the situation.

This means that communication is freed from the situation where it happens to take place. Now, for example, the woman could comment on the beauty of the pictures after she has left the house. Or, simply by dropping the article *the*, she could distinguish between the beauty of the specific pictures before her ('The pictures are beautiful') and the beauty of pictures in general ('Pictures are beautiful').By varying the tense of the verb, she could distinguish between pictures which *are* there now, *were* there yesterday, *will be* there tomorrow, and so on. She could even shift her whole perspective and talk about pictures which, at some previous time, *had been* there.

(4)   Through the grammar, communication is now liberated not only from the physical context where the speakers happen to find themselves but also from concrete events themselves. As well as talking about what really *is*, *was* or *will be* there, the woman could talk about what *is not* there ('It would be nice if we had some pictures here'). Or she and her friend could delve beneath the surface of reality and reflect on *why* things are as they are. In other words, language now provides the tools for almost limitless imagination, speculation and analysis.

Through the grammatical system of the language, then, communication can become increasingly independent of its setting. Unlike the speech of infants or the foreigners' initial attempts to communicate, language can convey meanings which have no direct connection with the immediate situation where communication takes place.

1.4   Grammar and the Goals of Language Teaching

It has sometimes been suggested that when we adopt a 'communicative' approach in foreign-language teaching, grammar can be ignored. However, the discussion in this chapter illustrates how the ability to make choices within the grammatical system is an essential prerequisite to using language for communication. It is therefore not a question of ignoring grammar but of conducting a careful analysis of its function in enabling speakers to communicate meanings. This analysis should help us to decide, for specific groups of learners, what degree of control of grammar is appropriate to their communicative goals.

In this section I will suggest, for one small area of grammar, how an increasing penetration into the grammatical system enables learners to make a wider and more creative range of meaning-choices.

1.4.1   Learning fixed items

We saw in section 1.3.1 that the simplest form of communication relies on fixed items in concrete situations: the foreigner looks up single phrases in a dictionary or the child cries 'teddy!'

In the early stages of a foreign-language course it is now quite common for students to learn to express simple communicative functions in this way. For example, they may learn how to ask for things in a shop by simply naming the object and adding 'please' or its equivalent:

> One packet of tea, please.
> Two kilos of potatoes, please.

Because the language forms are presented and practised within a clearly-defined 'shopping' situation, it is obvious that they are to be interpreted as 'requests to buy', even though the learners only have to choose between singular and plural forms.

Communication without grammar can also take place through whole sentences, which are learnt as unanalysed wholes, as if they were items of vocabulary:

> How are you?
> I don't understand.

Sentences such as these can be learnt without any knowledge of the grammatical rules that underlie them. In the early stages of acquiring their mother tongue, children learn a large repertoire of such phrases to satisfy important 'survival' needs. The foreign-language 'phrase-book' is based on the same principle.

1.4.2   Learning slot-and-filler patterns

The first step towards using whole structures in a creative way occurs when students have to choose between alternative items to fill one or two slots in an otherwise fixed piece of language. For example, let us say that students have already learnt fixed items for food and drink, so that they can either request them ('A cup of coffee, please') or offer them to other people ('A cup of coffee?'). It is only a small step in complexity to fit the items into a longer stretch of language, which has also been learnt as a set pattern:

> Would you like a (cup of coffee)?
> Would you like a (piece of cake)?
> *etc.*

The students have not yet reached the point where they have to make choices within the grammatical system itself, since they only have to insert alternative lexical items into a fixed pattern. However, they now have the first tools for a limited form of creativity within a clearly defined situation.

We could go further and give the learners alternative phrases for the second half of the 'adjacency pair' (see section 2.3.2). They are then equipped to take part in a complete exchange:

Would you like a ... ?
– Yes, please.
or – No, thank you.

– but, even now, the communication does not depend on their using the actual grammatical system.

If learners move through a whole sequence of functional objectives of this kind – 'asking for food and drink', 'making offers', 'accepting and declining offers', 'asking the way' and so on – they will achieve at least a limited communicative ability for coping with a predictable range of situations.

For some learners this kind of communicative ability may constitute the final goal, since they may not have the time or the need to acquire more than a repertoire of items which will enable them to survive in the foreign environment. This is also the kind of communicative ability that often results, intentionally or otherwise, when objectives are defined narrowly in terms of separate communicative functions.

1.4.3 Communication through the grammatical system

For many learners the kind of communication just described is too rigid and restrictive to constitute a goal in itself. They want to learn to use the language creatively, in order to express personal meanings and understand the unpredictable language that other speakers direct at them. For this they have to gain access to the underlying system of the language, so that they can not only use set phrases or insert alternative words into fixed patterns, but also make choices within the grammatical system itself.

If we consider the nature of these systematic choices, we can see that they lie among a continuum, stretching from purely lexical choices (as in the previous section) to choices which operate deep inside the grammar. Here is a simple illustration of this continuum. It is not given as a proposed teaching sequence but only to show how increased degrees of access to the grammatical system open up increased possibilities for communicating meanings.

Level 1 A learner can use only fixed phrases which have been memorized in association with fixed meanings:

Would you like a sandwich?

With this phrase, obviously, the learner can offer a sandwich but nothing else.

Level 2   The learner can insert alternative noun phrases into the final slot:

Would you like a (sandwich)?
Would you like a (cup of tea)?

This gives her a limited ability for creativity: she can now offer any object which the grammar classifies as 'countable'.

Level 3   The learner can select other elements within the noun phrase, such as different articles and adjectives:

Would you like (a sandwich)?
Would you like (some jelly)?
Would you like (the chocolate biscuit or the cream biscuit)?

She is no longer restricted to one type of object. She can also distinguish between alternative objects (e.g. types of biscuit) which differ only in minor details.

Level 4   The learner can choose between a noun phrase and a verb infinitive to fill the final slot:

Would you like (a sandwich)?
Would you like (to dance)?

She can now ask her partner whether s/he is interested not only in objects but also in activities. The communicative function shades over from 'offering' towards 'inviting'.

Level 5   If the learner combines the new ability to choose between a noun phrase and a verb infinitive with the old ability to manipulate choices inside the noun phrase, more possibilities open up:

Would you like   (a sandwich)?

Would you like (to see)   (some photographs)?
Would you like (to buy)   (these cakes)?

This ability to choose different verbs as well as different nouns extends dramatically the number of utterances that the learner can create and understand.

Level 6   So far the choices have all affected the second half of the utterance. The learner now moves into the first half and makes choices which affect the tense of the main verb:

(Would) you like (these cakes)?
(Do)   you like (dancing)?
(Did)   you like (seeing) (the photographs)?
(Will)   you like (the sandwiches)?

Since she can combine these new choices with the ones she was making in level 5, her communicative repertoire undergoes a further large expansion. She can now ask about her partner's likes and dislikes in general and in the past.

Level 7   When the learner makes choices in the subject of the main verb:

(Would) (you) like (to see) (the photographs)?
(Would) (he)   like (to buy) (the cakes)?
(Does) (he)   like (dancing)?
(Did)   (they) like (the sandwiches)?

– she can ask for the same information in relation to other people.

Level 8   When she chooses between different main verbs:

(Does) (he)   (like)   (dancing)?
(Did) (he)   (dance)?
(Did) (you) (eat)   (the sandwiches)?

– she can talk about other phenomena than just people's 'likes and dislikes'.

Level 9   When, in addition to all the grammatical choices that were mentioned in earlier stages, she can also select between interrogative and declarative verb forms:

> (Did you eat) (the sandwiches)?
> (You ate)   (the sandwiches).
> (They liked)   (seeing) (the photographs).

– and between affirmative and negative forms:

> (She likes)   (dancing).
> (I don't like) (these cakes).

– the learner possesses a flexible, creative system for conveying an immense variety of meanings about her world in the present, past and future.

We have taken just one area of language as an example of how, as learners increase the number of choices they can make at different points in the grammatical system, they extend also the range of meanings they can express and understand. Far from the grammatical system being irrelevant in a communicative approach, then, just the opposite is true: the more deeply a foreign-language learner penetrates into this system, the more effectively he or she can communicate.

2 Meaning and Interaction

2.1 Introduction

One reason why it is useful to begin by considering communication separately from language, as we did in chapter 1, is that this helps us to highlight an important fact: in communication we are 'doing things' with words (cf. Austin, 1962). At the simplest level we might simply be doing what could easily have been done without using words at all (clapping hands = 'stop talking'). At more complex levels we use the full resources of the grammar to convey subtle distinctions and ideas (cf. Halliday, 1985). However, we are still basically 'doing things' with words: when we convey a meaning to somebody, we cause some change in that person's mental world. This change may or may not cause that person to 'do something' (with or without words) in response.

In this chapter we will look a little more closely at the meanings that language can express and how they are exchanged when people interact with each other.

2.2 Three Kinds of Meaning

To illustrate the kinds of meaning that we communicate through language, I will start from a situation similar to the one described in the last section:

> A woman stands in a room, points to an empty wall and says to her friend: 'It would be nice if there were a picture there.'

In these words we can distinguish three levels of meaning which are being conveyed simultaneously. They are labelled in different ways by different writers (cf. Coulthard, 1983; Graddol et al., 1987; Lyons, 1981; Yule, 1987). Here I will call them 'literal meaning', 'functional meaning' and 'social meaning'.

2.2.1   Literal meaning

In the words spoken by the woman, there is one level of meaning where she is simply making literal reference to concepts and ideas shared by all adult speakers of the language. We all have an idea of what kinds of object are usually described as 'pictures'; we know that 'nice' is a label for general approval; we understand 'would be . . . if' to refer to a situation which does not yet exist but could do; we assume that 'there' indicates a place known to the speaker; and so on. These are the conventional meanings that would be listed in a dictionary or grammar. Even if we came across the words printed out of context, we would be able to understand them at this literal level.

The woman and her friend can attach a more precise literal meaning to the words by virtue of being in the situation together. For example, they know what the word 'there' refers to; the nature of the place might give additional hints about the type of picture; and so on.

In most everyday situations, this literal level of meaning (which is often also called 'propositional' or 'referential' meaning) is clear and hardly open to disagreement. Provided the woman and her friend share a minimum of linguistic and cultural knowledge, there should be little difficulty in their achieving a meeting of minds at this level.

2.2.2   Functional meaning

However, words are not only a vehicle for the meeting of minds. They are also embedded in a flow of social interaction and have a purpose (a 'communicative function' or 'functional meaning') within this interaction.

The woman could have a variety of different communicative purposes when she utters the words. Here are just a few:

- She might be suggesting that her friend could buy a picture to go on the wall.
- She might be asking him (or preparing to ask him) to fetch a picture from the next room.
- She might be reproaching herself for getting rid of the picture that used to be there.
- She might be hinting that a picture would be a suitable present for her next birthday.
- She might simply be passing a casual comment in order to make polite conversation.

The woman's purpose could be a mixture of more than one of these. For example, she could be simultaneously reproaching herself (for selling the picture) and suggesting that her friend could buy another.

In most circumstances we would expect the participants to share enough knowledge of the situation and each other for the man to interpret the words in the way(s) the woman intended. However, the possibility of misunderstanding is always present. For example, let us say that the woman is soon to have a birthday and her friend thinks she has an over-acquisitive nature. In this case he may well interpret her words as a veiled request for a birthday present, even though she only intends them as a casual remark. Unless this misunderstanding is cleared up by the conversation that follows, both participants might remain unaware of it, causing the man to be reinforced in his unfavourable opinion of the lady and, perhaps, leaving the woman to wonder why her friend has become colder towards her. There is no way of knowing how often this kind of mismatch between intention and interpretation occurs in daily social life or how often it is the cause of problems in social relationships.

We can see, then, that whereas the words are fairly straightforward when we have to interpret them at the literal level (as in 2.2.1), they become more problematic as soon as we have to interpret their functional meaning. The latter can only be determined when we take into account the situation where communication takes place and the relationship between the participants. Even then, there may be room for disagreement.

2.2.3   Social meaning

In 2.2.2 we took an utterance as our starting point and saw that it could be used to express a variety of communicative intentions. In this section we will take a communicative intention as our starting point and see that it can be expressed by a variety of utterances. Here is an adapted version of the example presented earlier:

> A woman stands in a room with her friend, looking at an empty wall. She wants him to fetch a picture from another room. She says . . .

Here are some of the ways she might choose to express herself, including the one we discussed in 2.2.1 and 2.2.2:

- Fetch a picture from the other room, please.
- Can you get a picture from next door, please?
- Would you mind fetching one of the pictures from next door?
- One of the pictures from next door would look good there.
- It would be nice if there were a picture there.

As we move down this list of possible expressions, the relationship between the words' literal meaning and their intended functional meaning becomes less direct and the hearer has to do more work to interpret what is intended. This means that there is more scope for misunderstanding. It also means, however, that there is more scope for negotiation. In the first two utterances the woman is requesting the man unambiguously, but with different degrees of force, to carry out the action she desires. If he declines to do so, there may be confrontation or, at least, some loss of 'face'. In the last two utterances, there is an easy escape-route: if the man does not wish to comply, he can draw a different functional interpretation from the words and guide the conversation elsewhere. The third utterance is somewhere in the middle: it is clearly a request but phrased in such a way as to leave some room for negotiation.

By expressing herself more indirectly, then, the woman takes more account of her friend's point of view. She enables him to feel he is being given a choice rather than direct instructions. It may also be that she is not yet fully convinced herself that moving the picture would be advisable: she therefore 'floats' the idea in an indirect way in the hope that the discussion that follows will help her to clarify her own ideas. In all of these ways, the choice of one form rather than another affects the force of the functional meaning and opens up varying degrees of scope for negotiation and exploration.

Requests belong to a special category of speech act in which one speaker is 'imposing' in some way on somebody else. Others include complaints, apologies and suggestions. With this kind of speech act there is a potential threat to somebody's 'face'. In the case of requests, for example, the receiver of the request may feel that his or her free choice is being constrained. In turn, the requester risks receiving a refusal. Not surprisingly, as Brown and Levinson (1978) have shown, language offers ways of negotiating these situations with the minimum of risk to face. In particular, the more formal the social situation is, or the greater the social distance is between the participants, the more likely it is that a speaker will choose a more indirect form of expression (e.g. the third in the list above, which is sufficiently clear to be understood but still sufficiently indirect to avoid offence in most situations). Mitchell-Kernan and Kernan (1977) have shown how people recognize these social conventions of language use at an early age: even a seven-year-old may take offence if a younger child expresses a request in a way that seems too direct.

Although it is with face-threatening acts such as requests that the need to match certain forms of expression with certain kinds of social situations is most obvious, social appropriateness is also important in other areas of communication. This is shown by the examples below, which are from a completely different domain of language use: a lecture about language teaching. The sentences listed on the left are from the *written* text of the lecture. Those on the right were produced when the lecturer came to actually *speak* her text:

The same can also be done with schools	You can do the same with schools.
To sum up:	OK, I think that's about enough, let's sum up.
More of that at the end of the paper.	I'll come back to that later on.
One might ask how one could be sure.	You can ask 'How can I be sure?'

When I have presented these sentences (and others from the same situations) in random order to native speakers or advanced learners, they have had no difficulty in determining which form was produced in which situation. Clearly they share with the lecturer a similar set of social conventions for language use, according to which some forms are more or less formal than others. Their correct responses also show how, through these conventional links with particular kinds of social situation, different forms of expression come to carry social meanings which speakers can interpret independently of any specific situation. Therefore, through the forms they choose, speakers convey information about how they perceive the social situation and their relationship with each other. If the speakers do not perceive the situation in the same way or if one of them misunderstands the social intentions behind what the other says, the threat to the interaction is as great as with other kinds of misunderstanding. Indeed it may be even greater, since people's self-esteem is at stake.

In the next section we will look at meanings in this broader context of social interaction.

2.3   Social Interaction

For the sake of simplicity, much of the discussion so far has presented communication as if it were simply a one-way process, with messages moving from speakers to hearers. However, in section 2.2 we also saw several times how the hearer's interpretation is an unpredictable but crucial factor in the interaction. So too, of course, is the hearer's response to this interpretation; and the original speaker's response to this response; and so on, *ad infinitum*. In other words, social interaction is a collaborative process in which both (or all) participants are creatively involved.

We can see this collaboration at work both in the exchange of meanings and in the ways that interaction is organized.

2.3.1   *Exchanging meanings*

Let us take another simple example:

Frank, Bill and John are sitting at a table in a restaurant where they have met to discuss the arrangements for their club's annual party. There is a pause.

Before anybody speaks, there is already a considerable degree of overlap between the mental worlds of Frank, Bill and John. For example, they share common knowledge of the situation they are in, why they are in it, their roles and their relationship to each other; they possess common cultural and general knowledge; and so on. Obviously there are also a lot of differences in the knowledge and assumptions that they bring, but here we are interested mainly in the common elements that make up their 'shared world' before the interaction begins.

> After a pause, John addresses Bill: 'I like that jacket you've got on, Bill.'

John's words focus all three participants on one particular aspect of this shared world. They also introduce into this world a number of new features, which correspond to the three kinds of meaning which we discussed in the previous section:

1   At the *literal* level of meaning, the words simply focus all three participants onto one particular aspect of the shared situation (Bill's jacket) and express the idea that John likes it.

2   At the *functional* level of meaning, John is making a communicative move to which the others will respond differently according to how they interpret it. For example, Frank may simply focus on the new information about John liking the jacket and indicate agreement or disagreement. Or he may think that John is being sarcastic (especially if he thinks the jacket is old) and tell him to be quiet. Bill himself may take it as a straightforward compliment and respond by thanking Jack. Or he may feel embarrassed, because he realizes that John knows he has borrowed it from a friend. And so on.

3   At the *social* level of meaning, the words may simply serve to indicate John's friendly interest in Bill's welfare. However, if they are interpreted as sarcastic, they might introduce tension or hostility. Or if John and Bill are not already well acquainted,

John's use of Bill's first name could be taken as an attempt to make the relationship less formal; and so on.

In this way new elements of various kinds are introduced into the shared world, through the combined effect of John's words and the others' interpretations of them. These interpretations lead to responses which, in their turn, introduce new elements into the shared world. And so the process continues: the conversation is constructed through collaborative activity, as the speakers introduce new meanings into their shared world, respond to them, clarify them, reject or expand on them, until the interaction comes to a close.

The important elements in the interaction are not only words. Signals are also being conveyed by participants who are silent (cf. Argyle, 1978; Ellis and Beattie, 1986): they may nod, smile, murmur 'yes' or 'mmm', and so on. These signals perform an important role in indicating that people are participating and – even when they are not speaking – still collaborating in the construction of the inter-action. If the signals fail to appear, this failure is itself a signal to the speaker that the listeners are no longer involved in the interaction, and feelings of discomfort often result.

2.3.2   Organizing the interaction

Another important aspect of this cooperative activity is the way in which the participants organize the interaction amongst themselves: who talks when, how a conversation is begun and ended, how topics are agreed on, and so on.

In some situations there are clear-cut rules for this organization. In a traditionally-organized classroom, for example, it is usually the teacher who distributes speaking-turns amongst the students, begins and ends the stages within the lesson and decides which topics are relevant (cf. Sinclair and Coulthard, 1975). Similar rules (but with more scope for flexibility) govern most formal interviews. In everyday conversations, the rules are less overt and the organization is less centralized, but there are none the less conventions which ensure (usually) some degree of predictability and order (see for example Coulthard, 1983; Graddol et al., 1987; Levinson, 1983).

In many situations a degree of organization is provided by so-called 'adjacency pairs'. These are simple exchanges in which the first utterance creates expectations for a particular kind of second utterance. Together the two utterances form a complete unit. Examples are:

(a) greeting + greeting: A: Good morning, Joan.
                                    B: Morning, Margaret.
(b) question + answer: A: What's the time, please?
                                    B: About 8.30, I think.
(c) offer + response: A: Want a biscuit?
                                    B: No thanks – they're too sweet for me.

Sometimes additional elements may interrupt the simple two-part sequence, but without destroying the basic structure. For example, the last example could have gone as follows:

A: Want a biscuit?
B: What kind are they?
A: Chocolate digestive.
B: Milk chocolate or plain?
A: Milk.
B: No thanks – they're too sweet for me.

Adjacency pairs are the basic building-blocks of conversation and, so long as the participants follow the conventions, they take care of much of the structure of simple interaction. However, this still leaves a lot of conversational activity in which coordination has to be achieved by some other means.

According to observational studies (reported for example in Coulthard, 1983, and Ellis and Beattie, 1986), there are a number of conventions and devices which help us to organize our conversations. The basic expectation, at least for English speakers, is that there will always be one person (but only one person) speaking at a time. There are certain cues which (especially if two or more of them occur together) indicate that the current speaker might be ready to give up the floor to somebody else. Examples are when he or she:

– completes a major grammatical unit (e.g. a clause or sentence);
– pauses;
– uses a 'sociocentric' phrase such as 'you know' or 'isn't it?';

- completes certain types of intonation pattern;
- uses certain types of hand gesture;
- drawls on the final syllable;
- lets his or her gaze rest on the hearer at the end of the utterance.

Conversely, a speaker who is *not* yet ready to give up the floor can defend it by avoiding these potential change-over points. For example, rather than pausing for thought *after* a completed utterance, he or she may first begin a new grammatical unit by using some kind of 'filler' phrase (such as 'so as you can see . . .'). As well as making it clear that the speaker proposes to keep the floor, this also gives time to formulate the next idea.

Listeners are not completely at the mercy of the speaker's willingness to give up the floor. They have devices of their own. For example, they may lean forwards slightly or utter certain formulae, such as 'yes, but . . .'. In the last resort, they may simply jump in very quickly when they spot a small potential change-over point (e.g. a completed phrase or idea). This is obviously an operation which may require a higher degree of opportunistic skill and control of language than many foreign speakers possess.

2.4   Conclusion

Richards and Rodgers (1986) point out that every approach to language teaching is based (implicitly or explicitly) on a theory of language and a theory of learning. The first two chapters in this book have been about a theory of language.

We can summarize the discussion so far by relating it to the three views of language that Richards and Rodgers distinguish in their book. Each view reveals important aspects of language and, taken together, they provide a composite perspective on language as a vehicle for communication.

2.4.1   The structural view of language

In chapter 1 we focused on the structural system of the language. We saw how language provides us with a system of 'signals' which enable us to convey meanings. It is possible to achieve a limited degree of communicative ability by simply learning some of the fixed items (words and phrases) from this system. However, if learners want to be able to communicate meanings flexibly and creatively, they have to learn to operate the system itself.

2.4.2   The functional view of language

In the first part of chapter 2 we focused on language as an instrument for 'doing things' in social settings. When we use language, we are not only interested in the literal meanings of the words but also in the communicative functions (or 'speech acts') that they express. We have to relate words to the wider situation in which communication takes place, in order to express and understand the intended functional meanings and (through the choice of alternative forms) the social meanings which the forms also carry.

2.4.3   The interactional view of language

Through language and the meanings it conveys, we engage in social interaction with each other. This interaction does not proceed as a rigid series of one-way messages but is the product of collaboration and negotiation. Within their 'shared world', which changes constantly as the interaction proceeds, people interpret, question, clarify and respond to each other's messages. They also have to organize this interaction and share out the available speaking time.

These three models of language offer different insights and perspectives on the nature of language use. At any one time, we can adopt one perspective in preference to the others, depending on what features we want to highlight. However, if our aim is to achieve a global view of what is involved in learning and using language for communication, we cannot ignore any of the features that the three perspectives reveal.

In some respects, the interactional view of language is fundamental to understanding the other two. It can even be seen as subsuming them and adding further dimensions of its own. Thus, it is as part of their social interaction with each other that people communicate the different kinds of meaning discussed in the first part of this chapter. In turn, the communication of these meanings depends on the system of linguistic signals discussed in chapter 1. In other respects, however, we can regard the structural view as fundamental: it is only through the grammatical and lexical system that we can express the rich variety of meanings which enable social interaction, as we know it, to take place. Fortunately we do not need to arbitrate on the relative importance of the three perspectives: far more important is the realization that all three exist in mutual dependence and that none can be properly understood except in relation to the others.

Part II Learning

Introduction

In Part II of the book we remain at the level of 'approach' but shift our attention away from the nature of language and onto ways in which language is learnt.

Chapter 3 adopts the perspective on learning that has dominated most recent approaches to language teaching. Language learning is seen as a form of skill-learning, in which the items to be learnt are isolated and presented separately to the students, who perform various kinds of practice activities in order to master them. Through a combination of 'part-skill practice' and 'whole-task practice', the students gradually internalize the mental plans that underlie skilled language use and learn to put these plans into operation fluently and correctly.

Chapter 4 adopts a contrasting perspective which has been the subject of a great deal of discussion in recent years. Language learning is now seen as a form of natural growth. This perspective derives from watching how children learn their mother tongue and how some people learn a second language naturally, as a result of being exposed to it in communication situations. In these cases, language is acquired without explicit instruction and the development seems to follow laws of its own. If we could understand these laws, they might offer us powerful new ways of organizing learning in the classroom.

Both of these kinds of learning take place in the real world and so both accounts contain truth within them. In trying to make classroom learning more efficient, it seems sensible to use all the learning capacities that people possess and, therefore, to try to exploit both their skill-learning and their natural-learning capacities. Chapter 5 considers how the two kinds of learning might be integrated into one framework, which can then form the basis for our methodology.

3 Learning Language as a Skill

3.1 Introduction

When foreign-language learning takes place in a typical school situation, it often looks like a process of skill-learning rather like, say, learning to swim or play the piano. To begin with, there are certain 'target skills' which exist independently of the learner and have to be acquired: structures, recalling vocabulary items, finding ways to express communicative functions, and so on. The teacher isolates these target skills for the learners and often explains them. The learners practise them in ways prescribed by the teacher. Their performance is evaluated according to how close it meets certain external criteria, such as accuracy or appropriateness.

If we move outside school and look at how a second language is learnt by young immigrants who have just arrived in a new country, it appears to be a completely different phenomenon. The language is not divided into separate components: right from the start, the learners experience it as a living whole. Nobody explains each item to them: they have to make their own sense of what they encounter. They are not required to practise specified parts of the language: they use whatever language they can find to express what they want to say. Other people do not evaluate the accuracy or appropriateness of their language: they respond to the meanings the learners express.

These two descriptions are a caricature of the two situations and, in reality, more overlap exists: in school there are some activities where the focus is on experiencing the language as a natural means of communication, and outside school there are often helpful people who provide explanations and corrections. In broad terms, however, the comparison is valid: in school situations, a lot of attention is paid to controlling the learning through organizing the way the language is presented and practised; outside school, language appears to develop naturally as a by-product of the learners' involvement in communication.

In this chapter we will look at some of the assumptions behind the first kind of learning mentioned above: language learning as a form of skill-learning.

3.2 Acquiring Cognitive Habits

In the second half of the 1960s there was a heated debate between the supporters of two contrasting views of the nature of language and language learning (for more details see Diller, 1978; Stern, 1983; Wilkins, 1972).

On one side of the debate were the supporters of the 'behaviourist' approach, associated especially with B. F. Skinner. As the term suggests, the behaviourists saw language as a form of behaviour. They saw behaviour itself as being composed of habits. Language learning is therefore simply a process of acquiring verbal habits. The conditions for acquiring these habits can be systematically controlled:

1 The language learners imitate speech that they hear.
2 This imitation is rewarded (e.g. by approval or some other desired response).
3 As a result of these rewards, the behaviour is repeated and becomes habitual.

In this way the learner's verbal behaviour is gradually shaped and comes to correspond more and more closely to the original model.

In the field of language teaching, the habit-formation approach to language learning provided the main principles for the audio-lingual and audio-visual methods which dominated many classrooms of the time. These are characterized by a large proportion of activities (such as the memorization of dialogues and the use of drills) which lead learners to repeat the same language patterns until they can produce them automatically in response to the appropriate stimulus (cf. Richards and Rogers, 1986; Rivers, 1964 and 1981). Similar techniques are still in widespread use today.

On the other side of the debate were the supporters of the 'mentalist' or 'cognitive' approach, of which the foremost proponent was Noam Chomsky. Chomsky and his followers pointed out that language is too complex to be explained in terms of behavioural habits. The actual verbal behaviour that we observe is only the 'tip of the iceberg'. In the human mind, underlying this behaviour, there is a system of rules. On the basis of this system, we can produce and understand sentences which we have never come across before, in order to meet the unpredictable demands of daily communication. This essentially creative aspect of language means that the most important aspect of language learning must be the development of an internal cognitive system; that is, an internalized 'grammar' of the language.

Polarized debates like this are common in the world of language teaching and, as in many other cases, this one led most of the participants to a compromise view. John Carroll (1971) summed up this compromise with the term 'cognitive habit-formation': yes, the basis for using language creatively must be a system of mental rules; but yes, too, if a person wishes to use the language fluently in communication situations, these rules have to be applied automatically, like a set of mental habits. Language learning involves developing a set of habits (i.e. automatized skills), but these skills have their basis in the mind.

3.3 Performing a Skill

This compromise view coincides nicely with accounts of other kinds of skilled performance, where it is generally agreed that both cognitive and behavioural aspects are involved (cf. Levelt, 1978; McLaughlin, 1987; Welford, 1976).

Underlying the effective performance of any skill is the ability to form 'cognitive plans' which direct the behaviour itself. These plans operate at different levels but are integrated when performance takes place. In ballroom dancing, for example, we can distinguish higher-level plans which determine what kind of dance to perform; middle-level plans which determine the dancers' direction and the precise sequence of steps as they move around the floor; and lower-level plans which control the specific movements of the limbs and their coordination with the music.

The cognitive plans that underlie skilled performance are linked in a continuous hierarchy so that, apart from the very highest and the very lowest, each plan is controlled by one at a higher level and depends in its turn on lower-level plans for its actual execution. We can see this in relation to language by returning to the example used in chapter 1, where a woman wants to get her friend to fetch a picture from the next room:

- At the highest level of the hierarchy there is the goal the woman wants to achieve: to get the picture into the room. This goal probably grows out of her previous preoccupations and/ or, more immediately, out of the ongoing interaction between herself and her friend.
- She must decide whether to fetch it herself or try to get her friend to do so. The two options will lead to completely different sub-plans, with only the second necessarily involving language.
- If the woman decides on the second of these options, she must choose between different ways of carrying out her communicative intention. These range from a direct order or request, through various kinds of indirect request, to more complicated strategies for getting the friend to make an offer himself.
- If she decides to make an indirect request, she must select an overall grammatical pattern which can express it appropriately. She must also select the lexical items to put into the pattern.
- Within the grammatical pattern itself there is a hierarchy of choices to be made. These determine the overall structure of the sentence, the construction of individual phrases, their sequence in the sentence, the tenses of verbs, morphological endings, stress, intonation, and so on.
- The actual production of the utterance involves a complex sequence of articulatory plans and motor skills.

The sequence just described agrees in outline with the model of language production developed by M. Garrett on the basis of various kinds of empirical evidence (cf. Garrett, 1982; also Harris and Coltheart, 1990; and Smyth et al., 1987). In this model, our cognitive processes cause speech to pass through four 'levels of representation' before it is actually produced as sound. First, conceptual planning-processes create the 'message level' at which ideas and general meanings are represented. Second, broad syntactic frames are assembled and word meanings are selected in order to create what Garrett calls 'functional level' plans. Third, the exact sentence-structure and word-forms (with endings etc.) are defined in order to create plans at the 'positional level'. Finally, plans are created for the actual articulation of the words. These plans result in the physical production of speech.

3.4   Adaptability and Automaticity

An important characteristic of the plans that produce skilled performance is that they can be adapted to changing circumstances. Let us say, for example, that two skilled dancers begin a complex figure but find another couple in their way. Even though the plan has been created and the dancers have begun to put the appropriate lower-level plans into operation, they are not obliged to carry out the original plan regardless of its consequences. They can adapt it or abandon it completely. If they do, all the lower-level plans for carrying out the figures will automatically be changed or cancelled in their turn.

This last sentence indicates a second important feature of many of the plans which underlie skilled performance: once they *are* selected, they operate automatically. Skilled performers possess a large repertoire of plans that are ready-made and, once selected, can unfold without conscious effort or attention. Thus, in the example above, skilled dancers would not need to devote conscious attention to the lower-level plans that control their physical movements: these, and the behaviour associated with them, would come into play automatically in response to choices at higher levels. The same would normally be true of the middle-level plans, though situations might arise where these have to be shaped consciously (for example, if the dancers set out consciously to try out a specific sequence of figures or if the dance-floor is so full that it becomes difficult to avoid other dancers). Otherwise, the couple can devote all their attentive capacity to higher levels and let the lower-level plans unfurl automatically.

Adaptability and automaticity are connected with each other. So long as the lower-level plans operate automatically, we can devote maximum attention to controlling performance by forming effective higher-level plans. We can also monitor what we are doing, assess whether the original plan still appears to be suitable as the situation develops (i.e. attend to 'feedback') and, if necessary, adapt it while the performance is in progress. Provided the lower-level plans are sufficiently automatized, any higher-level changes will pass down immediately to the lower levels and into the performance. For example, if a skilled dancer chooses to produce a 'natural turn' instead of an intended 'reverse turn' (in order to avoid a collision), the changed plan will automatically be transmitted to the lower levels and result in a different sequence of body movements.

When we use language, we are constantly having to create new higher-level plans at the level of ideas, meanings and conversational strategies. The effective execution of these plans depends on a high degree of automaticity at the lower levels. For example, in the course of a discussion conducted at normal speed, it would be completely impossible to devote conscious attention and effort to the construction of every sentence: this must occur automatically in response to the ideas we want to express at specific moments. Equally, we must be able to adapt our plans as interaction proceeds. To take two simple examples:

> I make a telephone call to a friend and the words of greeting ('Hello, Margaret, I'm just phoning to see how you're getting on') are already in my mind. But the call is answered by a man. I must quickly substitute a more appropriate plan and put it into immediate execution ('Hello, is Margaret there, please?').

Or:

> I prepare to tell a friend the news that Fred Jones is getting married: 'By the way, you know Fred Jones?'. The friend replies 'Yes – he's getting married, you know.' I must immediately adapt my original plan, which was to say exactly those same words.

3.5　Learning to Perform a Skill

Compared to skilled performers, novices are limited in two main areas:

1　They have less knowledge about what plans to select for achieving different objectives.
2　They do not possess a large repertoire of ready-made plans which can be put into operation automatically.

As a result they have to apply more conscious attention to creating and performing plans at lower levels. In the case of language learners, this means that they may have to devote much more conscious effort than native speakers to constructing sentences, selecting vocabulary items, inflecting words or producing difficult sounds. Since their attentive capacity is limited (cf. Levelt, 1978; McLaughlin, 1987), they often have to make a sacrifice: when they devote a lot of attention to the higher levels of meaning, they may have to sacrifice the fluency and/or accuracy of their language; alternatively, when they devote a lot of attention to the accuracy of the language-production processes, they will have less attention to devote to higher-level domains such as the formulation of ideas or the monitoring of their partner's responses. Their ability to communicate will be particularly hindered when they are tired, nervous or under pressure to respond quickly.

Within this framework, there are three main aspects which belong to the learning of a skill:

1　Learners have to become aware of the key features of the target performance, so that they can create the mental plans which are necessary for producing it themselves.
2　They have to practise converting these plans into actual behaviour, so that in due course the lower-level plans can operate automatically, in response to higher-level decisions.

These two aspects of learning develop the cognitive and behavioural dimensions necessary for individual components ('part-skills') of the total skill. The part-skills of communication that learners practise might include producing grammatical structures, pronouncing new sounds, selecting vocabulary items, expressing specified communicative functions or using devices for managing conversations (e.g. 'conversational gambits' as in Edmondson and House, 1981).

3 They must learn to start from a higher-level plan (e.g. an idea or a reaction) and select lower-level plans which are appropriate for carrying it out. For example, language learners must become capable of producing particular structures or selecting particular items of vocabulary not only as part of a controlled activity in which their focus is on the items in question, but also in response to a particular communicative intention which arises, unpredicted, during interaction.

This component is sometimes called 'whole-task' practice. It requires the various part-skills to be integrated into a systematic network, so that the performer can select whichever ones are needed in order to carry out the plans conceived at higher levels. In the case of foreign-language learning, a learner must be able to produce language while his or her primary focus is on the communication of meanings.

In the terminology used by Rivers (1975, 1983), the first two components of learning listed above make up the 'skill-*getting*' stage of language learning and the third is the 'skill-*using*' stage. In the terminology of Littlewood (1981), the first two components constitute the 'pre-communicative' stage while the third is the 'communicative' stage. This terminology should not, of course, be taken to imply that the stages follow each other in a neat sequence. At any one time during a course, there is likely to be a balance of part-skill and whole-task practice, with the emphasis shifting more and more onto the latter as learners progress. Nor should we conceive of the stages as being clearly distinct: the one shades imperceptibly into the other. For example, we shall see in section 5.4 how a communication task may be structured in such a way that it lies on the borderline between part-skill and whole-task practice.

3.6 What Goes Wrong in Performance?

From the discussion in the previous sections, we can summarize some of the reasons why a language learner's performance may be less efficient than he or she would like it to be. Such diagnosis can often be useful in deciding what treatment is needed in order to improve the performance.

1   The most obvious failure in performance occurs when a learner conceives a communicative purpose for which his or her language repertoire simply does not contain the lower-level plans needed for carrying it out efficiently. The result may be:

(a)   The learner has to abandon the original purpose or simplify it in some way. This not only places obvious limitations on the learner's scope for expression but can also have detrimental effects on his or her confidence. If such occasions occur frequently they can contribute to a sense of reduced personality and language shock (cf. Larson and Smalley, 1972; Brown, 1980).

(b)   The learner tries to create alternative plans for solving the communication problem. This may involve using gestures, paraphrase or any of the other 'communication strategies' which foreigners have been observed to use (cf. Faerch and Kasper, 1983) and which are sometimes taught explicitly (cf. Bialystock, 1990; Buckby, 1989; Tarone and Yule, 1989).

These two alternatives correspond to what Faerch and Kasper (1983) term 'reduction strategies' and 'achievement strategies' in foreign language communication. It is clearly advantageous to learners' performance if they can be helped to develop the skills and confidence to use strategies of the second kind.

2   A further source of weakness is when a learner's repertoire contains the necessary lower-level plans to carry out a desired communicative intention but these plans are not yet sufficiently automated to operate without conscious attention and effort. This can have a variety of results, such as:

(a)   Learners try to put together plans while they are performing. For example, they give conscious attention to verb endings or word order while they are actually producing a sentence. Or, if circumstances permit, they try to work out what they want to say before they actually say it. This may make their performance halting and wearisome to listen to. It also reduces their ability to respond quickly in conversation and to adapt to changing circumstances.

(b)   If there is no time to put plans together consciously or if they have insufficient attentive capacity (e.g. due to pressure or tiredness), plans from different sources may interfere with each other as performance takes place (cf. Levelt, 1978; Littlewood, 1984; McLaughlin, 1987). For example, native-language plans may get mixed up with foreign-language plans, leading to so-called 'transfer' or 'interference' errors. Alternatively, two or more foreign-language plans may become mixed, leading to so-called 'overgeneralization' errors.

To remedy these shortcomings, the learner needs more practice in converting plans into performance at the part-skill level as well as in whole-task contexts.

3   A learner may have a large number of individual automated plans in his or her repertoire. However, he or she has not had sufficient whole-task experience to be able to select and adapt the plans appropriately to particular communicative purposes as these arise during interaction. As a result:

(a)   The learner may be able to produce a wide range of language items so long as communication takes place in certain predictable, everyday transactions. Outside these situations, however, the learner may not be able to retrieve the same items in order to express unpredicted meanings during interaction with other people.

(b)   The learner may be able to use a range of structures in the form that he or she has internalized them but cannot create new combinations of low-level plans in order to express new meanings. For example, the learner may not have developed sufficient flexibility to take elements from 'I should see . . .' and 'I have seen . . .' and create 'I should have seen . . .'

This ability to retrieve plans in response to higher-level demands and to adapt plans to suit immediate needs can only be developed through whole-task practice, in which learners are required to move through all the stages of production outlined by Garrett (1982) in his model (cf. section 3.3 above): from conceptual planning to the actual articulation of speech.

3.7   The Role of the Teacher

When language learning is viewed as a form of skill-acquisition, the role of the teacher is similar in principle to that of the instructor for most other kinds of skill.

1   In the first place, the teacher has to divide the total skill into manageable components ('part-skills') and order them in such a way that the learners will be able to master them in sequence. In language teaching these operations of 'selection' and 'sequencing' are usually regarded as belonging to the field of syllabus design (cf. Nunan, 1989). Obviously, however, they also have an important influence on how we try to teach in class.

2   The teacher has to provide the learners with a model of the performance they are expected to produce in a particular part-skill and make them aware of the essential features of this performance, so that they can produce it themselves. In language teaching this corresponds to what we often call the 'presentation' phase (cf. Byrne, 1986; Hubbard et al., 1983).

3   The teacher has to organize controlled activities in which the learners practise performing part-skills (i.e. converting lower-level cognitive plans into actual behaviour). In the terminology of language teaching this is what we often call the stage of 'controlled practice' (Hubbard et al., 1983), 'pre-communicative activity' (Littlewood, 1981) or 'skill-getting' (Rivers, 1975, 1983).

4   The teacher also has to create contexts which will provide learners with opportunities to integrate the various part-skills that they have learnt so far and perform the 'whole task'. In language teaching this is the stage of 'free practice' (Hubbard et al., 1983), 'communicative activity' (Harmer, 1983; Littlewood, 1981) or 'skill using' (Rivers, 1975, 1983).

An essential element in stages (3) and (4) is that the learners should receive some kind of feedback (either during or after the practice) so that they know how close their performance comes to the target they are aiming to achieve. Whereas in stage (3) the feedback is often likely to focus on formal features of the performance such as its accuracy, in stage (4) there is more likelihood that the

feedback will focus on the extent to which the learners have suc-
ceeded in communicating their intended meanings. Both kinds of
feedback are possible at every stage but the dominant trend is currently towards greater focus on meanings rather than on form (see
for example Hughes, 1989; Lee, 1989; Underhill, 1987).

This trend towards greater focus on meanings has been strongly
reinforced by the growth of interest in the other model of language
learning mentioned in the introduction to this chapter: the natural-
acquisition model. It is to this model that we turn in chapter 4.

4 Language Learning as a Natural Process

4.1 Introduction

The conception of language learning as a natural process has its starting point not in the classroom but in the natural environment, where learning occurs without formal instruction. As with the skill-learning model, it focuses on the mental system that underlies the use of language, but it is a mental system of a different kind. It is not now a system which begins as external to the learners and which the learner is expected to internalize in ways prescribed by an instructor. Rather, it is a system that the learners develop for themselves, as they use their own powers of observation and generalization to make sense of the language they experience. As a result of their involvement in communication, the language seems to grow inside them by natural processes.

4.2 'Creative Construction' in First-Language Learning

The initial impetus for looking at language learning as a process of natural growth came from studies of how children acquire their mother tongue. We saw in section 3.2 how, in the 1960s, many psychologists and linguists came to challenge the behaviourist view of language learning as 'habit-formation' and emphasized that learning must consist in developing rules for creating and understanding new utterances. In their search for evidence to support these views, many researchers began to make intensive studies of early language development in children (cf. Brown, 1973, and later surveys in Crystal, 1986; de Villiers and de Villiers, 1979; Harris and Coltheart, 1990).

These studies led to the view that natural language learning is a process of 'creative construction'. On the basis of what they hear, children 'construct' rules of their own to account for the regularities in the language. These rules constitute the children's internal 'grammar', which begins as a very simple system but gradually develops until it is the same as the grammar of adult speakers of the language. However rudimentary this grammar may be at the start, children can use it (like adults) to create sentences they have never heard and to express their own meanings.

Here, for example, are sentences that a child created in order to ask for more of some object or activity:

> More page. (= 'carry on reading')
> More sweetie. (= 'give me another sweetie')

– and to comment on something she could no longer see:

> Allgone milk. (when the bottle was empty)
> Allgone outside. (when the door was shut)

In learning to form questions or negatives, children construct the underlying rules in a sequence of stages. For example, a normal sequence for learning to construct negatives is:

1   'No' is placed at the beginning of a sentence (e.g. 'no singing song');
2   'No' is placed inside a sentence (e.g. 'he no bite you');
3   A negative particle is placed after 'can', 'do', etc. (e.g. 'you don't want some supper').

One of the clearest illustrations of how children are actively involved in constructing rules is the way they acquire certain irregular verb forms. Very early in their development, they give the impression that they have mastered the correct past tense forms of many irregular verbs:

> He did it.
> He went home.

Later, however, they appear to forget what they have learnt and use incorrect forms:

> He doed it.
> He goed there.

However, this apparent step backwards is really a sign of progress, because at this time the children have formed a *general rule* for talking about the past. They can now be creative with past tenses and, for example, derive 'he walked' from 'walk' and 'he played' from 'play'. This same rule makes them derive 'doed' from 'do' and 'goed' from 'go', until the time when they learn that there are exceptions to their rule. Then they go back to using the correct forms 'did' and 'went'.

When we look at language learning in terms of developing grammars, it is no longer appropriate to talk about 'errors' in the normal sense (cf. Corder, 1981). As we have seen in the examples above, children produce a large number of forms which do not correspond to the forms that an adult would produce. However, they are a reflection of the children's grammatical system at that point in time rather than simply imperfect attempts to match the adult's system. This view that errors are a natural element in the learning process has had considerable influence in the field of foreign-language learning.

4.3   Creative Construction by Second-language Learners

The perspective on language learning that emerged from studies of first-language acquisition stimulated people to look for evidence of similar processes in second- and foreign-language learning. They found this evidence in two main areas: in the sequences that emerge when children or adults learn a second language in a natural setting and in the kinds of error that foreign-language learners make in class.

Many similarities have been found between the sequences involved in natural second-language learning and those found in first-language acquisition (cf. Cook, 1991; Ellis, 1985; Hatch, 1978; Littlewood, 1984; McLaughlin, 1987). For example, second-language learners often use a simplified system of their own as a means of communicating meanings:

Ball doggy?
He champion.

As a further example, the typical sequence in which second-language learners acquire negative forms in natural settings is similar to the one that children follow:

1   First, a negative particle ('no', 'not' or later 'don't') is placed before the verb (e.g. 'I no sing it', 'I don't can explain').
2   Later, the negative particle is placed *after* some of the more common auxiliary verbs, such as 'is' and 'can' (e.g. 'somebody is not coming in').
3   Eventually, learners use some form of 'do' in order to show the person and tense, and place the particle after it, as in correct native-speaker usage (e.g. 'it doesn't spin').

Many other similarities have been found between first- and second-language learning. The main extra dimension, as one might expect, is that second-language learners sometimes transfer rules from their first language. For example, the form 'John like not that' is typical for German learners, for whom it corresponds to the first-language pattern, whereas Spaniards often reflect their own first language by placing 'no' before the verb for a longer period than other learners.

The above examples are taken from learners in natural settings but there is evidence that in classrooms, too, learners are trying to make their own sense of the language they are exposed to. This is shown most clearly by the errors they make (cf. Corder, 1981; Ellis, 1985; Littlewood, 1984). Often these show learners transferring rules from their mother tongue, as for example in the case of a French speaker who uses a tense that would be appropriate in her native language:

I know London since 1985.

Often the errors show learners overgeneralizing rules within the foreign language itself:

They goed home.
He is not wanting it.

Forms such as these show how foreign-language learners, like first-language learners, construct rules creatively rather than simply modelling the forms that are presented to them. They also show how these natural processes of rule-construction are often more powerful than the learning processes that teachers try to control.

The power of natural learning-processes emerges clearly from a study that was conducted in Germany (Felix, 1981). The researchers observed a series of lessons in which schoolchildren were taught how to use interrogative and negative forms in English. They also observed the forms which the learners actually produced, in order to find out whether these forms were closer to (a) the ones they had been taught in their lessons or (b) the ones which natural learners usually produce at a similar stage of learning. They found that the classroom learners often followed the 'natural' sequence more closely than the sequence which the teacher had tried to impose. For example, even after they had been thoroughly drilled in correct interrogative forms like 'What are they picking?', 43 per cent of the forms they produced themselves were uninverted ('What they are picking?'), like those used by natural learners at this stage. In other words, the classroom learners were more inclined to follow their own 'built-in syllabus' (Corder, 1981) than the external syllabus devised by the teacher.

4.4 What are the Conditions for Natural Language Learning?

If natural learning-processes operate in classrooms (whether we want them to or not), it would obviously be better to try to make them work *for* our teaching rather than against it. Unfortunately, the very fact that they operate in natural, uncontrolled situations means that we have little definite information about the precise conditions that stimulate or hinder them. The most that we can do is to examine some of the features that seem to be present (or absent) in situations where natural learning takes place.

The most obvious characteristic that these situations all share is that the learners are involved in real communication through the language. This fact alerts us immediately to some of the conditions that do *not* need to be present for natural learning to take place:

1   The language does not have to be presented in a graded
    sequence such as we usually find in schools. The learners are
    exposed to natural samples of the language.
2   There is no need for the learners to practise actually producing
    every language item. They develop their linguistic competence
    by processing internally the language they hear.
3   There is no need to correct the language that the learners
    produce. Their grammar develops spontaneously in the direc-
    tion of the native-speaker system.

What is more difficult is to decide what features *are* essential, since
it can always be argued that even if any particular feature had been
absent, language would have developed just the same. One example
of this is the question of whether it is necessary to actually speak the
language in order to construct a grammatical system or whether
language can be acquired through listening alone. One argument is
that since we can often understand speech without processing the
grammatical details (e.g. by using context), it is only through actually
speaking that learners will attend to these details and construct their
internal grammar (cf. Swain, 1985). The counter-argument is that
acquisition requires only 'comprehensible input' and that, once an
internal grammar has been constructed, speaking skills develop spon-
taneously (cf. Krashen, 1985). In arguments like this, a lot depends
on exactly how we define key terms such as 'acquisition'. Can we
say that language has been 'acquired' even before a person can
produce it? If so, how do we know *what* the person has acquired,
since we have no direct access to his or her internal knowledge? It
is not easy to see how questions of this sort can be resolved.

Bearing these difficulties in mind, we can try to distinguish some
of the conditions that seem to be necessary in order for successful
natural learning to take place.

(1)   The most obvious condition is that there must be some kind of
exposure to language input, so that the natural learning-mechanisms
have something to work on. Although this language does not have
to be exactly graded to suit the learners' level, they must presumably
be able to attach meanings to it, in order to sort out the relationship
between language items and their function in communication. Krashen (1982, 1985 and elsewhere) uses the term 'rough tuning' for
the way that speech addressed to foreigners is often simplified to

enable them to cope with it better (e.g. through clearer pronunciation, slower pace, simpler structures and common vocabulary). Also, for younger learners in particular, the speech is often easier to understand because it is closely related to the immediate situation.

As I mentioned above, Krashen argues that the resulting 'comprehensible input' is the necessary and sufficient condition for stimulating natural language acquisition (see for example Krashen, 1982, 1985; also the summary and a critique of his theory in McLaughlin, 1987).

(2)   Many writers (e.g. Long, 1985) believe that it is interaction with other people, rather than simple exposure to language, that plays the most crucial role in enabling acquisition to take place. When learners interact with others, they are able to influence the kind of language that they are exposed to. For example, they can ask for clarification and repetition, indicate difficulties, raise or avoid topics, and generally ensure that it is more suited to their level and interests. In addition, during interaction two speakers often build up utterances together over a number of turns, so that the learner is helped to construct sentences which were previously outside his or her capability. This process of 'scaffolding' may be an important help to the learner in internalizing the structure of the language (cf. Hatch, 1978).

(3)   Since natural learning depends on the learner's active mental engagement with the language, motivation is an important factor. In language learning, motivation derives first and foremost from the need to communicate with others. In studies of first-language learning it has been shown how communication between mother and child provides the initial contexts for the growth of language (cf. Bruner and Haste, 1987). Likewise it is clear from looking at the contexts where second-language learning takes place successfully that the need to use the language for communication is a crucial factor. For example, immigrants who try to integrate with their host communities learn much more of the language than those who remain in their own 'enclaves' (cf. Schumann, 1978). Conversely, observers of children in French 'immersion' classes in Canada have suggested that natural learning often proceeds only to the point where learners have acquired enough French to satisfy their communicative needs (cf. Harley and Swain, 1984).

(4)   The example of immigrant learners points to a second aspect of motivation which a large number of studies have identified as a key factor in second-language learning: the learner's attitudes to the second-language community. This is a more generalized kind of 'communicative need', which exists independently of specific situations and draws the learner towards the language as the means for contact with a valued social group. Many studies have found that this so-called 'integrative' orientation towards the other community is one of the most powerful factors in successful learning (see Gardner, 1985; Skehan, 1989).

(5)   The learner's attitude towards the second-language community is often classified as one of several emotional (or 'affective') factors which influence the process of learning. These also include how the learner feels within the learning situation itself. Gardner (1985) found in various studies that 'situational anxiety' is an important factor in language learning. Outside the classroom, people often use the terms 'language shock' or 'culture shock' to refer to the feelings of insecurity that can arise when people are deprived of their natural means of communication and find that their familiar frames of reference are no longer valid (cf. Brown, 1980). The converse of this is that a relaxed situation and a network of supportive personal relationships encourage learners to engage their whole selves in the learning experience.

So far as we can tell, then, two of the essential conditions for natural language learning relate to the provision of adequate learning opportunities: exposure to the language and interaction with other people. Two are connected with motivation: a need to use the language in real communication and a more generalized desire to make contact with the people who speak the language. The last condition concerns the extent to which the learner's emotional state enables him or her to be open to the new learning experiences.

4.5   Conclusion

The account that I have given here of natural language learning can be summarized in figure 4.1.

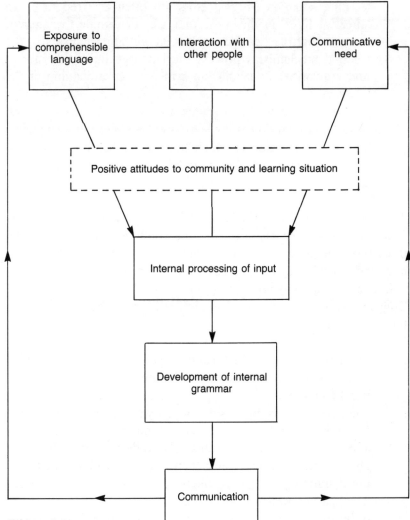

Figure 4.1

Moving from top to bottom:

- The three basic conditions of natural learning are exposure to the language, interaction with other people (which may include interaction through the written language), and the need to communicate.
- The effect of these conditions is facilitated or hindered by the learner's attitudes to the second-language community and the

learning situation (these factors are often referred to as an 'affective filter' in the sense that they determine the amount of input that reaches the internal learning mechanisms).

- Internal mechanisms process the language input in order to find regularities and build up a mental representation of the language.
- This representation constitutes an internal grammar, which continues to develop as the learner experiences more language.
- The internal grammar which the learner has constructed at any particular time enables him or her to take part in communication.

The process represented in figure 4.1 is circular, since 'communication' at the bottom also provides the conditions described in the three boxes at the top: exposure, interaction and the need to communicate. In this way the process is self-propelling.

By way of comparison, a diagram of the skill-learning model of language learning is presented in similar terms in figure 4.2. From top to bottom:

- Input is provided in the form of separate learning items which correspond – one hopes – to the learner's objectives in following the course.
- The effect of this input is modified by the learner's motivation (including attitudes to the other community) and by his or her aptitude for language learning. (Aptitude is often believed to affect formal learning more than natural learning, but this is not definitely proven – cf. Skehan, 1989.)
- The learner practises the language that has been taught in order to internalize it as 'cognitive plans'. The practice usually involves the performance of part-skills (e.g. separate structures or functions) as well as the whole task (communication).
- The skills become increasingly automated so that lower-level operations can unfurl without conscious attention.
- Communication takes place by means of automated plans and (if the situation allows it) less-automated plans to which the learner must still devote a degree of conscious attention.

In this model of learning, 'communication' at the bottom does not feed back into the top of the diagram (as it did with natural learning) but into the middle box as 'whole-task practice'.

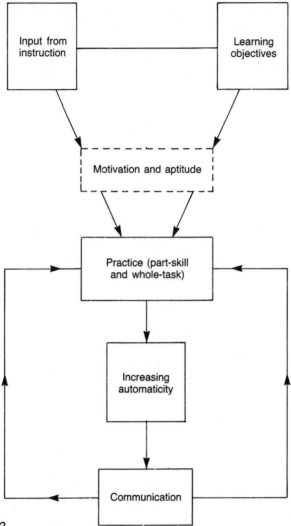

Figure 4.2

In the next chapter we will consider how these apparently conflict-ing forms of learning might be integrated so that classroom learning can benefit from them both.

5 Integrating Skill-learning and Natural Learning

5.1 Introduction

In chapters 3 and 4 we were confronted with two models of language learning. According to the first (chapter 3), language learning is a form of *skill-learning*. It is associated with controlled activities for practising pre-selected items ('part-skill training') which lead to more independent forms of practice in using language for communication ('whole-task practice'). According to the second model (chapter 4), learning is a natural process of 'creative construction' and is associated with situations where language develops naturally, through exposure and use.

These models are so different that our first reaction might be that one must be 'right' and the other 'wrong'. Yet experience shows that both kinds of learning can provide the basis for developing communication skills in another language. When we come to consider teaching a foreign language for communication in the classroom, therefore, our first task must be to decide what kind of contribution each kind of learning can make.

5.2 One Model to the Exclusion of the Other?

One possible response to the two models of learning is to use just one as the basis for teaching and exclude the other completely.

In support of using the skill-learning model as the sole basis, we can argue that the classroom is a special kind of situation which cannot provide the conditions necessary for natural learning; that in any case, natural language learning takes a long time and is inefficient; and that we should therefore try to cultivate the special kinds of controlled learning that the classroom *can* support more effectively. As Widdowson (1990) has pointed out, this is a normal response in the case of many other forms of school learning. It is also the approach adopted by most widely-used teaching methods of recent years, such as the audio-lingual method (Brooks, 1960) or situational language teaching (Davies et al., 1975). With their emphasis on controlled practice and helping learners to avoid making errors, these methods try to protect learners from their own natural inclinations, so that they can be led along the paths fixed by the syllabus.

On the other hand it can also be argued, mainly on the basis of observations outside schools, that language learning is fundamentally different from other kinds of classroom learning and will occur most efficiently if we concentrate on enabling learners' natural processes to operate. In this case our main aim in the classroom should be to create contexts where learning can take place through natural communication. There is in fact a long tradition, reaching back beyond Roman times, of learning foreign languages through communication alone (cf. Howatt, 1984). More recently, the renewed interest in studying natural language learning outside the classroom has provided the theoretical basis for several teaching approaches. For example, Krashen and Terrell (1983) argue in favour of a 'natural' approach which consists almost exclusively of techniques for stimulating communication, and Prabhu's 'procedural' approach (1987) involves the learners mainly in solving problems which are presented through the foreign language. In both approaches there is little or no controlled practice or correction: learners are left to 'acquire' the foreign language in the same way as they have acquired their mother tongue. The proponents of both approaches provide evidence that they have been successful in the situations where they have been used (with adults in the USA, in the case of the 'natural approach'; with adolescents in India, in the case of the 'procedural approach').

Both the skill-learning model and the natural-learning model have thus provided the foundations for teaching approaches which have been successful in the classroom. However, neither has led to the almost universal success which (from what we know about human language-learning capabilities) we ought to be able to achieve. The reasons for this may lie not so much in the models themselves as in our attempts to turn them into practice: it is possible that, 'around the corner', we will discover ways of either harnessing people's skill-learning capacities, or re-creating in classrooms the essential conditions for natural learning, which will bring classroom foreign-language learning within everybody's reach. However, since this has not occurred yet, we need to explore the other possibility: that each kind of learning has its own useful contribution to make in the classroom and that we should therefore look for ways of integrating them within a broader framework.

We will turn to that possibility in the next section.

5.3 Integrating the Two Kinds of Learning

What we are looking for, then, is an overall framework which will enable us to assign a function to both kinds of learning. This can then form the basis for an approach to teaching in which both kinds of learning can make their contributions to the learners' progress.

5.3.1 'Learning' and 'acquisition'

One framework which has won a lot of attention in recent years is the 'Monitor Model' of Stephen Krashen (e.g. 1981, 1985). This model solves the question of integration by assuming that we possess two sets of language-learning mechanisms which operate separately from each other. One set of mechanisms enables us to learn in a conscious way: to learn rules, memorize vocabulary, benefit from drills, and so on. A different set enables us to learn in a natural, subconscious way. Krashen uses the term 'learning' for our conscious processes and 'acquisition' for our subconscious processes. I will follow the same convention in this chapter.

Krashen argues that it is the system of language that we acquire by natural processes that underlies our ability to communicate. The system which we consciously learn plays only a subordinate role: it enables us to 'monitor' what we produce and increase its accuracy. The practical implication that Krashen draws from this is that language teachers should devote most of the available classroom time to creating situations in which natural acquisition can take place –

in other words, situations in which the learners can use the language for communication. The 'natural approach', mentioned above, proposes ways of doing this.

In Krashen's framework the two sets of processes feed into two completely different systems which are not linked. This means that items which have been learnt consciously cannot pass into the 'acquired' system. A number of writers have criticized this view (e.g. McLaughlin, 1987). It runs against the intuitions of most language learners and, as Rivers (1980) has pointed out, there is little evidence in other areas of psychology to support the idea of two learning systems existing as totally separate. It is more normal for mental systems to form networks and interact, in ways which cognitive psychologists have now begun to illuminate (cf. Anderson, 1985; Bialystock, 1990; O'Malley and Chamot, 1990). Krashen's account is therefore frequently adapted to allow for links of some kind between the two systems, such that items which have been learnt consciously can later enter into the acquired system (e.g. as a result of practice). From here, together with items that have been acquired through natural communication, they can become available for spontaneous communication.

This last sentence touches on another element of Krashen's model that many people do not accept: his proposal that only the subconsciously 'acquired' system can be used for communication. 'Consciousness' is an elusive phenomenon which cannot be measured objectively and exists in varying degrees rather than 'completely or not at all' (cf. Sharwood Smith, 1981). However, many people feel confident that they often apply conscious as well as unconscious knowledge to the task of communicating through another language (cf. Rivers, 1980; Gregg, 1984). For example, they sometimes prepare what they want to say in advance; put sentences together consciously as they speak; analyse mentally some of the difficult sentences they hear, in order to work out their meaning; or use conscious communication strategies to overcome problems that arise. It seems counter-intuitive to claim that, in situations such as these, we are not using conscious knowledge for the purpose of communication.

In figure 5.1 I have taken Krashen's model as the starting point but adapted it in the two ways just indicated, in order to represent the proposed relationship between conscious learning and natural acquisition. This figure shows two main routes by which learners can internalize language:

1 consciously, through traditional forms of instruction based on the skill-learning model, and
2 subconsciously, by engaging in communication through the language.

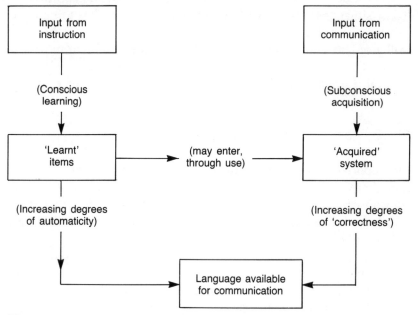

Figure 5.1

The fundamental difference between the results of the two kinds of learning is characterized by Sajavaara (1978) as follows:

1 Conscious learning provides rules which can at first be applied only with conscious effort and which, therefore, the learner needs to automate by means of practice.
2 Subconscious acquisition provides rules which are already automated when they enter the learner's communication system.

However, as the consciously-learnt material becomes more auto-mated through practice, it enters into the same 'internal store' as material that has developed in the learner through natural processes. At this point, therefore, items which have been automated through instruction and practice have the same status in the learner's mental/

linguistic system as items which have developed as a result of natural learning.

At any given point in time, items which have been learnt, but not yet automated, can still contribute to communication, provided the learner can devote enough attention to using them. However, in many situations – particularly when communication has to be fluent – a learner will not have enough attention-capacity to use them and will need to communicate solely through the acquired/automated store. This will lead to a greater proportion of errors, in which the natural learning sequences illustrated in chapter 4 will be evident.

5.3.2   Learning and communication

An important implication of the preceding discussion is that there are different ways in which what has been learnt – whether consciously or subconsciously – can contribute to communication (cf. Bialystock, 1990; McLaughlin, 1987). When learners communicate, they have different kinds of rule at their disposal:

1   rules which have emerged in an already automated form, as a result of natural acquisition (many of these will not correspond to the rules of native-speaker speech but will gradually develop in that direction);
2   non-automated rules which have recently been learnt and can only be used accurately in favourable situations (e.g. when there is not much stress and learners have time to devote a lot of attention to lower-level grammatical processes);
3   rules which were initially learnt consciously but have become automated as a result of frequent practice and use, so that learners can use them fluently even when their attention is on the higher levels of meanings.

Types (2) and (3) are the two ends of a continuum along which there are rules of varying degrees of automaticity, depending on factors such as how often they have been used and, perhaps, the extent to which they are supported by similar structures in the native language or by the learner's natural developmental schedule.

These different kinds of rule can be pictured as different language 'stores'. When learners communicate, they draw on these different stores and use items of various kinds: items which have been taught but still demand attention; semi-automated items which are used correctly in some circumstances but not in others; and items which can be used in any situation, because they are fully automated (this does not necessarily mean they are 'correct', however, particularly if they are the result of natural acquisition processes). Fluent communication is favoured when as many items as possible have entered this automated store (through practice or as a result of natural acquisition), so that maximum attention can be devoted to the higher levels of meaning.

One implication of this account is that a learner's communication system will often possess more than one version of what we would otherwise call 'the same' linguistic structure. For example, it may simultaneously contain the 'correct' way of forming negatives (which has been learnt through instruction) and an 'incorrect' way (which the learner had acquired naturally). According to the constraints of the situation, the learner will produce sometimes one version, sometimes the other, perhaps sometimes a form which combines elements of both. This is one reason for the wide degree of variability that has been observed to occur in the speech produced by language learners (cf. Tarone, 1988).

5.3.3 Conscious learning as a reinforcement for natural learning

We saw in the last paragraph that 'learning' and 'acquisition' can cause the learner to possess two different forms for the same function: one 'correct' but not yet automated, the other acquired (and therefore already automated) but 'incorrect'. Eventually, given appropriate experiences, the two lines of development should meet:

- As a result of practice, the correct form should become increasingly automated.
- As a result of natural sequencing, the acquired form should evolve in the direction of the native-speaker model.

The fact that people are able to learn a new language through a combination of instruction and natural exposure is evidence that some kind of convergence like this takes place, though its exact nature must remain a matter of conjecture. So long as the two lines of development are separate, however, it seems likely that they may interfere with each other, since they will often provide the learner with conflicting lower-level plans for expressing the same meaning.

The possibility that rules learnt from instruction may interfere with rules acquired naturally is addressed by Pienemann's 'teachability hypothesis' (1985, 1989). In one study, Pienemann taught a new structure to two groups of Italian learners of German. One group had reached a stage in their development where, according to the sequences observed in natural learning, they were ready to acquire the new form. The second group had not yet reached this stage. Pienemann found that instruction helped the first group to acquire the new structure more quickly. However, it simply left the second group confused. From this and other evidence (including the study by Felix, 1981, mentioned in section 4.3), Pienemann argues that a new language structure is only 'teachable' through explicit instruction if it is taught at a time when the learner's natural processing mechanisms are ready to receive it. In this case teaching can serve to accelerate the rate at which the new language structure is acquired. If on the other hand the learner's natural mechanisms are *not* yet ready, explicit teaching and formal practice can be not only ineffective but even detrimental, since they work against the natural course of development.

There are a lot of unknown factors in these studies. For example, we know nothing about the quality of the teaching in relation to the capacities and learning styles of the learners: it may simply be that the teaching was inadequate. We also have little information about whether (as the account in 5.3.1 would suggest) the taught structures *were* used correctly in situations where the learners could attend to their production. The teachability hypothesis does, however, encourage us to follow a path which common sense would also suggest: to try to organize courses in such a way that formal practice activities support, rather than contradict, the sequence of learning that comes naturally to the learners. The latter can, however, be exposed to other structures in a more unfocused way, as part of the language input which they experience in the course of natural communication (cf. Pienemann, 1985).

Further studies of natural sequences may help us to coordinate conscious and natural learning in a more systematic way than is possible at present. In the meantime they can be useful in reminding

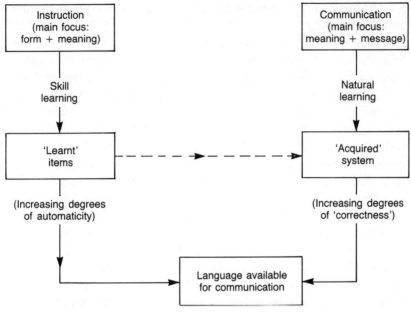

Figure 5.2

us that, at any particular stage of development, some structures are likely to be beyond a learner's capacity for automatic control and are best left to develop later in the course of natural progression.

5.4   Learning and Teaching

We can now look at some of the pedagogical implications of the discussion in this chapter. For the sake of convenience I will relate them to a diagram which I have adapted from the one presented in figure 5.1.

The left-hand side of figure 5.2 focuses on language learning as a skill-learning process. The main input to this process comes through organized instruction in which we pre-select the items (e.g. sounds, vocabulary, structures or communicative functions) that we ask the learners to internalize. These items may be of varying kinds, ranging from ready-made routines such as 'Can I help you?', through patterns with slots to be filled, such as 'Would you like to . . .?', to deeper-level choices such as the distinction between the present continuous and the simple past.

In terms of the skill-learning model, these items are all cognitive 'plans', but they differ greatly in the extent to which they can be adapted and transferred to new situations. Thus, of the examples just given, 'Can I help you?' is a fixed item which serves one very specific communicative intention in an equally specific interpersonal context; 'Would you like to . . .?' is more adaptable and can serve a wider but still limited range of intentions; while the choice between different tenses is an operation which can express meaning-choices in a wide range of contexts. It is the ability to operate a large number of plans of this last kind that enables a person to take part in unpredictable communication. This point was discussed in section 1.4.

If we manage to select items which the learners are ready to process in any case at their current stage of development (cf. 5.3.3 above), we can expect these plans to become automatic with little effort, since the process is supported by natural learning mechanisms. Otherwise, learners must have opportunities to use the plans until they gradually become automated and can unfold fluently. This process is represented by the bottom of figure 5.2: through practice, plans become increasingly automated and thus available for fluent use.

The amount of practice needed will vary widely, of course, according to factors such as the learners' aptitude and motivation, the complexity of the plan, how vulnerable it is to interference from other plans, and so on. Until a particular low-level plan is sufficiently automated to be used without conscious attention, there will be many communication situations where the learner cannot use it accurately.

As well as 'part-skill practice', in which individual items are isolated for separate practice, learners also need 'whole-task practice', in which they have to integrate a variety of plans in order to communicate a range of meanings. There is, however, no strict borderline between part-skill and whole-task practice, since the one shades gradually into the other. This can be illustrated by an example of a simple progression from obvious part-skill to obvious whole-task practice.

(1)   At the first stage in the continuum, let us say that some learners are asked to practise a specified item without actually communicating any new meanings to each other. For example, they may practise the present continuous tense by describing what the teacher is doing or

they may ask for objects (as if they were in a shop) when the teacher prompts them by holding up pictures.

At this stage they are obviously practising only the part-skills of communication. The main focus is on the forms of the language and on the *potential* meanings they can convey in future communication, rather than on actual messages being exchanged with another person. We can refer to this here as 'pre-communicative' work.

(2)   At the next stage they use the same items but the activity is now organized so that there is some communication of new meanings. For example, they may describe a picture so that somebody else can reproduce it or they may ask for objects in order to find out whether another person has them in his or her 'shop'.

There are now actual messages to be exchanged and, in that respect, the activity constitutes a limited form of communication. Since the meanings and language are controlled and predictable, however, we would probably hesitate to call it whole-task practice. Here I will call it 'communicative language practice'.

(3)   Let us say that the description of the picture now requires the learners to make a wider range of grammatical choices, or that they have to ask for the objects in the course of a role-playing activity where other items of language also occur. However, the learners can still cope by using only items which they have recently learnt and they do not have to cope with the additional demands of real-life situations, such as competing for speaking time.

Since there is now less predictability and a range of language is needed, we have moved further into the domain of whole-task practice. However, the learners are still protected from the full demands of communication outside the classroom. I will call this 'structured communication'.

(4) Let us now assume that the learners are given a communication task in a situation which has not been specially structured and where the meanings to be communicated arise freely out of the ongoing interaction. They are therefore likely to need to communicate meanings through language which has not been specifically prepared and under time-pressure similar to that outside the classroom.

We have now moved considerably further into the domain of whole-task practice, and the learners must integrate their knowledge

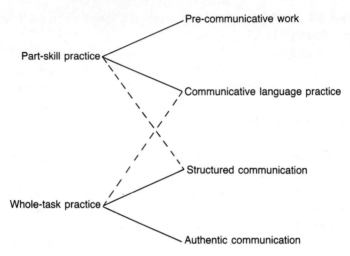

Figure 5.3

and skills in ways similar to those required in authentic communication situations. I will refer to this kind of work as 'authentic communication'.

The four kinds of work just described can serve as the main reference points for our methodological framework. We should remember, however, that they represent points along a continuum and cannot be sharply differentiated from each other in practice. This is illustrated in figure 5.3.

The right-hand side of figure 5.2 focuses on language learning as a natural process. The methodological implications of this model are in principle more straightforward than those of the skill-learning model. The task of the teacher is simply to create environments in which learners can communicate through the language and obtain the kind of input that is needed for natural learning to take place. The natural-learning model thus serves to highlight the importance of communication (receptive as well as productive) in the overall framework:

1   From a skill-learning point of view, it is 'whole-task practice', in which learners are able to integrate plans from different levels.
2   From a natural-learning point of view, it is the context in which

the learners' natural mechanisms can operate on language and construct their own system.

We can highlight the role of natural learning by adding it to the methodological framework as in figure 5.4.

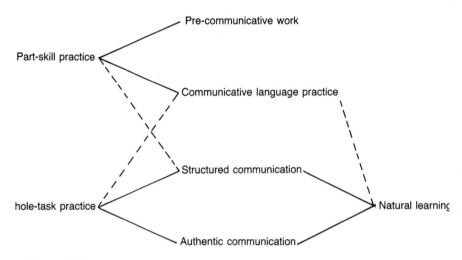

Figure 5.4

5.5 Conclusion

In the book so far we have examined the nature of communication and how language serves it. We have also looked at different kinds of language learning and how their respective contributions can be integrated for classroom learning. In the next chapter we will put together these views of communication and learning, in order to look a little more closely at their implications for classroom teaching.

Part III Teaching

Part III Teeeping

Introduction

Part I has provided us with a view of language as a system for enabling communication to take place. Part II has provided a view of learning which integrates learners' conscious, skill-learning capacities and their capacities for subconscious, natural learning. Thus we now have at our disposal the theories of language and language learning which, together, can constitute an 'approach' to teaching language for communication.

In Part III we move away from the level of 'approach' and into what Richards and Rodgers (1986) call the level of 'design'. We examine some of the implications of the first two parts of the book for the design of a methodology for teaching language in the classroom.

Chapter 6 is an attempt to draw up a framework for classroom methodology which takes account of the structural, functional and interactional aspects of language. It also aims to give scope to both kinds of learning. The purpose of the chapter is not to prescribe a methodology but to suggest a conceptual framework in which different activities can be related to each other and to the goal of language learning.

Chapter 7 adopts a different perspective on the language classroom. Rather than looking at relationships between activities, it takes a more global look at methodology and considers some of the features that must permeate it if the learners are to be fully involved in the learning that goes on in the classroom: opportunities for learners to take active roles, a sense of relevance, an emphasis on processes rather than products, and a supportive atmosphere.

6 A Methodological Framework for Teaching Oral Communication

6.1 Introduction

We have seen in previous chapters that learning to communicate means internalizing a set of 'cognitive plans', which learners can use in order to convey and receive meanings in specific situations. These cognitive plans may consist simply of short, fixed routines for performing useful communicative functions – many courses for 'survival competence' aim to provide learners with these. For the more creative kinds of communication that take place during social interaction, however, they need to be more flexible and involve grammatical choices.

We therefore need a methodological framework which will enable learners to internalize plans of increasing flexibility and relate these plans to meanings which become increasingly personal and creative. This framework must provide learners both with 'part-skill practice', in which individual components of communicative ability are isolated and practised separately, and with 'whole-task practice', in which these components are integrated in communication. At the end of Chapter 5 I sketched the rough outline of such a framework. In the present chapter I will propose a more detailed framework which is constructed around (a) the same kind of progression from part-skill practice to whole-task practice and (b) different kinds of meaning that learners need to express.

Figure 6.1 presents the framework in diagrammatic form. It will be explained in the course of the chapter. This framework is not proposed here as a prescriptive methodology but as a kind of conceptual map for linking different activities and relating them to the goal of communicative ability. Individual teachers will emphasize different parts of the map.

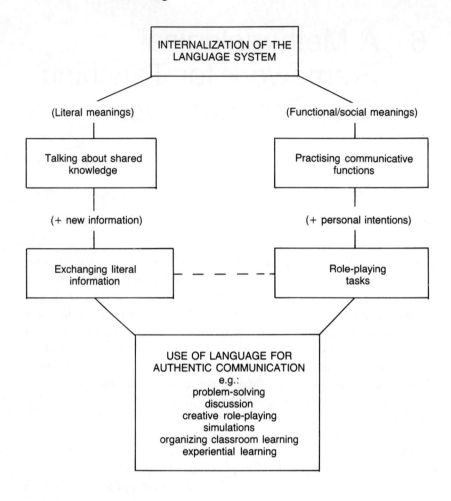

Figure 6.1

6.2   Structure of the Methodological Framework

The top and bottom boxes in the framework in Figure 6.1 describe two aspects of the goal towards which the activities must lead: the language system has to be internalized and it has to become available for the communication of meanings. At the same time these boxes are potential components of the methodology for reaching this goal:

many activities focus directly on aspects of the new language system and many other activities engage the learners in authentic communication. In between these two boxes are components whose function is to help learners to form links between language and the meanings it expresses.

In the following sections I will follow the general classification of activities into part-skill and whole-task practice, bearing in mind that as we proceed further in the whole-task direction, we are simultaneously providing opportunities for natural learning processes to take place. In the part-skill components in particular, I will also classify them according to whether they focus primarily on literal meanings or functional meanings. (The expression of functional meanings also implies the expression of social meanings, because the latter are present as soon as a specific form is selected from the alternatives available – cf. chapter 2.)

6.3 Part-skill practice

6.3.1 Internalizing the language system

As I said above, the idea of internalizing the language system can be understood in two senses. In one sense it characterizes the goal of all language-learning activities, whether they are part-skill or whole-task practice: they all contribute towards the learner's gradual internalization of the foreign-language system so that it can be deployed for purposes of communication. In another sense it describes a component of the methodology for achieving this goal: some activities focus specifically on the system of the language and aim to help the learner to master it.

In many traditional approaches a large part of the learning time is devoted to mastering aspects of the language system: learning and practising different tenses, inflexions, pronoun-forms, sentence patterns, and so on. Most of the exercises used in the grammar-translation approach, for example, are aimed at enabling learners to understand rules and apply them to constructing sentences. In the drills that became popular with the audio-lingual approach and which, with many variations (cf. Hubbard et al., 1983), are still widely used today, the main emphasis is on manipulating language patterns so that the learners can produce them fluently. More recently, too, some interesting discovery-based approaches to grammar have been developed (cf. Bowers et al., 1987; Shepherd et al., 1984), which encourage learners to work out for themselves how particular features of the language system work. In all of these cases, the focus is on the top component of the diagram presented in figure 6.1: on internalizing elements of the language system and learning to use the corresponding cognitive plans with increasing automaticity.

The emphasis on communication as the goal of language teaching has led some teachers to deny that grammar-oriented activities can play a role in their methodology. There is little justification for this, since linguistic competence is so obviously a central component of communicative competence (cf. Canale, 1983; Prabhu, 1987; Tarone and Yule, 1989) and since, after all, the new grammar and vocabulary constitute the main body of unknown material for a foreign-language learner (cf. James, 1983). However, there is justification for insisting – in view of the function of grammar in communication – that active links are maintained between grammatical choices and the meanings they convey (e.g. in drills: cf. Cook, 1982; Dakin, 1973; Ur, 1988), so that the linguistic system can more easily be integrated into the learners' communicative system.

The central goal of the other components of the methodology is to extend and deepen these links.

6.3.2   Linking language with its literal meanings

The first kind of meaning with which language must be linked is what we called in chapter 2 the 'literal' or 'propositional' meaning that an utterance contains: the ideas, facts or concepts that it refers to, irrespective of the specific communicative intention that leads the speaker to utter it on a particular occasion.

6.3.2 (a)   *Talking about shared knowledge*   The most widespread set of techniques for helping learners to link language forms with their literal meanings is familiar to us under labels such as 'situational language teaching' or the 'structural-situational' approach (cf. Davies et al. 1975; Richards and Rodgers, 1986). The common feature of these techniques is that the learners are asked to focus on some situation or area of knowledge that they share and to use the new language in order to describe it. The information that the language carries is therefore already familiar to everybody.

For example, the learners may be asked to describe the classroom situation in which they find themselves:

> Teacher: Where's John sitting?
> Student: He's sitting near the window.
> *etc.*

– or a picture:

> Teacher: Describe the scene in this picture.
> Student: (Describes the scene orally or in writing.)

– or the contents of a text they have read:

> Teacher: How many bears did Goldilocks find when she woke up?
> Student: Three.
> *etc.*

– or indeed any other kind of shared knowledge:

> Teacher: What's the capital of France?
> Student: It's Paris.
> *etc.*

These techniques have often been criticized for being artificial and 'uncommunicative': because the learners are providing information that everybody knows already, they are not performing acts of communication (cf. Widdowson, 1978). This is undoubtedly true when we consider the language activity only in terms of whether it is 'communication' or not. However, the ultimate criterion for judging the usefulness of language activity in the classroom is not whether it is communication but whether it helps people to *learn* to communicate. One important aspect of learning to communicate through a new language is that the new forms have to be integrated with the learner's existing system of concepts. These must often be adapted, in their turn, in order to take account of new distinctions expressed by the foreign language. For example, the German learner of English has to distinguish habitually between 'continuous' and 'non-continuous' actions; the English learner of German has to distinguish between two kinds of 'knowing'. The 'situational' techniques just described are one important means of facilitating this integration, since they leave learners free to match the forms of the new language with familiar aspects of reality, without imposing the need to cope with communicative acts.

6.3.2 (b)   *Exchanging literal information*   The dimension that is missing in the kind of activity just mentioned is the need to convey new information for a communicative purpose. This dimension is introduced when, instead of focusing on information that learners already share, we distribute information amongst them and give them a reason for exchanging it.

In order to illustrate the continuity between this component and the previous one, I will build on the examples already given.

With the first example in the previous section, we assumed that everybody in the class knew already where John was sitting. Let us now assume that only one student knows this (e.g. from a picture labelled with names). Another student has to find out the information, in order to identify the various characters in an unlabelled picture.

With the second example, we assumed that the picture was visible to everybody. Let us now assume that only one student can see it and has to describe it, so that another student can reproduce it or complete an unfinished picture. Alternatively, it may be one of a series of pictures, which the other student has to place into the correct sequence.

With the third example, we assumed that everybody had read the full story. Let us now say that only one student has read it and the others are involved in asking him or her about the details, in order to be able to reproduce it themselves.

With the final example, the fact that Paris is the capital of France is knowledge shared by all. Let us now say that a number of facts are not common knowledge and only one student possesses them. For example, they may be about some little-known country or about the student's personal life. The student must convey them to somebody else so that the latter can complete a table or carry out a survey.

In each of these cases, we are still concerned with the literal level of meaning. There is no question of the hearer needing to decide, for example, whether 'John's sitting near the window' should be interpreted as a warning, a complaint or some other communicative act: its function is simply to transmit literal information about his location. However, it now carries meaning that is new to the hearer and that the hearer requires. To that extent, the students are now performing communicative acts through language and the links between forms and meanings have become closer.

In recent years a wide repertoire of techniques has become available for creating the so-called 'information gap' that necessitates this exchange of information amongst learners (see for example Byrne, 1986, 1987; Harmer, 1983, 1987; Johnson, 1982; Littlewood, 1981; Revell, 1979).

6.3.3 *Linking language with functional and social meanings*

The second main kind of meaning that we discussed in chapter 2 was that of functional meaning. This level takes us firmly into the domain of language use as social interaction. We are interested not only in the literal meanings that speakers are conveying but also in the communicative acts that they are performing.

Because there is no one-to-one link between language forms and communicative acts, the same functional meaning can usually be expressed by a variety of forms and the same forms can be interpreted differently in different situations. In addition, a speaker's choice of language in a particular situation will carry information about how he or she interprets the social situation, especially in terms of its degree of formality. The functional level of meaning is therefore closely linked to the third level discussed in chapter 2: that of social meaning.

6.3.3 (a) *Practising communicative functions* This type of activity was introduced into communication-oriented courses as part of the reaction against the 'situational' techniques described above. Rather than practising language which is 'artificial' because it carries information already known, students practise language which is more authentic because it performs particular communicative acts (see for example Abbs and Freebairn, 1977; Scott, 1981). For example, they might practise how to make suggestions, corresponding to pictures or other cues given by the teacher:

Teacher: (Shows picture of a cinema)
Student: Shall we go to the cinema?

Teacher: (Shows picture of swimming bath)
Student: Shall we go swimming?

The connection between the functions and the context might be reinforced by asking students to picture themselves in a particular situation, for example, in a street where they ask each other how to get to various places marked on a map:

Student 1:   Can you tell me the way to the station, please?
Student 2:   Yes. Go straight on and turn third right.

The students are practising making conventional links between communicative intentions and language forms. The language use is still a long way from 'communication', however, since it does not express the students' own communicative intentions.

6.3.3 (b)   *Role-playing tasks*   When we were discussing the links between language and literal meanings in section 6.3.1, we saw that students move a step closer to the conditions of real communication when they become involved in conveying new meanings to their partners. The equivalent progression with functional meanings is when the students begin to express communicative intentions that are their own rather than determined by the materials or teacher. One of the functions of role-playing tasks is to provide contexts in which this progression can take place (see for example Byrne, 1987; Littlewood, 1981; Livingstone, 1983; Sturtridge, 1981).

There is not one single, unambiguous point at which we can say that students are expressing 'their own' communicative intentions. Rather, it is a continuum. At the beginning of this continuum is the kind of controlled role-playing task that is one of the mainstays not only of many courses organized around communicative functions but also of many examination systems (e.g. the GCSE in England and Wales: cf. Bird and Dennison, 1987):

You are in a baker's shop.

1   Greet the baker.

2   Ask for six rolls.
3   Ask how much they cost.
4   Ask the baker if s/he has change for a ten-pound note.
5   Say thank you and goodbye.

Here the communicative intentions are specified in detail and in origin they are clearly not 'the students' own'. Students can *make* them their own if they succeed in identifying with their role, but this is unlikely to occur in the majority of cases.

We move a little further along the continuum when we give students more scope to create their own communicative intentions:

You are going to a baker's shop. Decide what you would like for breakfast.

1   Greet the baker.
2   Ask for what you want.
3   If what you want is sold out, ask for something else.
4   Finish the transaction and leave.

This looser framework provides students with more scope to interact through personal meanings of their own, and thus to become more personally involved in the communication.

6.3.4   Literal and functional/social meanings combined

We can combine the principle of role-playing with the principle of information-exchange discussed earlier.

For example, the role-playing context might be a travel agency or booking office, in which one student is a customer who has to find out information for planning a journey and another student has the necessary timetables and price-lists.

This is comparable to activities based on interviews or questionnaires. In these activities, the 'roles' which the students adopt are their own, the 'context' is the actual classroom where they are learning, and the information which they have to exchange is real information about each other.

With these types of activity, then, we bring together the two strands

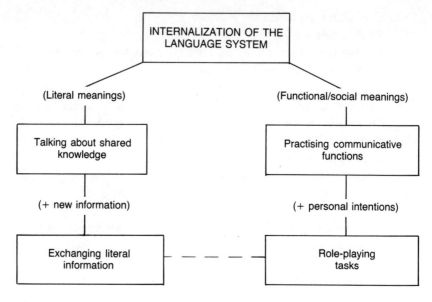

Figure 6.2

of part-skill practice: the one which builds on literal meanings (6.3.2) and the one which builds on functional/social meanings (6.3.3).

6.3.5   Summary of 'part-skill' components

Within the overall category of 'part-skill practice' we have now located within our methodological framework the various kinds of learning activity which make up the top two-thirds of the diagram presented in figure 6.1: see figure 6.2. This classification of activities is not clear-cut. Those in the top half of the diagram involve little communication and are most clearly within the domain of part-skill practice. To use other terms: they are what Rivers (e.g. 1975, 1987) calls 'skill-getting' as opposed to 'skill-using' activities; or they belong to the category of 'pre-communicative' rather than 'communicative' activity (Littlewood, 1981). The bottom half of the diagram is on the borderline. It has been classified here as part-skill practice, because the activities are usually carefully structured so as to avoid the unpredictability of normal communication. However, they also involve considerable focus on the communication of meanings and, in some instances, will lead to autonomous interaction between learners.

Depending on the degree of control, the activities belong to the categories described at the end of chapter 5 as 'communicative language practice' or 'structured communication'. They constitute an important bridge to facilitate the transition between 'part-skill' and 'whole-task' practice.

6.4 Whole-task Practice

As I have just indicated, we cannot draw an arbitrary line which defines where part-skill practice ends and whole-task practice begins. There is a gradual progression from very controlled activities at one end to completely free communication at the other. Along this progression there are varying degrees of control over the language and the meanings that are expressed. As we progress further towards the whole-task end of the continuum, so the interaction becomes less tightly controlled by external sources (such as the teacher or the materials) and springs more from internal sources, namely, the meanings that learners themselves decide to express at different stages of the interaction.

It follows from this that it is ultimately the learners themselves who determine where an activity lies along the continuum. For example, we may organize a role-play in which the course of the interaction is controlled by detailed cues (as with the first example in section 6.3.3(b) above) and which would appear therefore to be a clear instance of part-skill practice. When the activity takes place, however, we might find that some pairs of students are treating the cues only as a starting point for their imagination and are creating their own interaction around them. They themselves are determining the nature of the activity and taking it into the domain of whole-task practice.

With these provisos, we can extend the framework outlined above so that it includes activities in which the learners can carry out whole-task practice and (from the natural-learning perspective) can extend their own underlying system for the foreign language.

6.4.1   Problem-solving and discussion

The simple exchange of information which was discussed in section 6.3.2(b) consisted mainly of fairly predictable sequences of language which was linked to concrete facts and situations. Intentionally, the learners were protected from the normal unpredictability of communication, which would require them to create meanings in response to the demands of the ongoing interaction.

This dimension of unpredictability is introduced as soon as we add an element of problem-solving to the activity (cf. Harmer, 1983; Littlewood, 1981; Maley, 1981; Ur, 1981). For example, in the picture-description activity described in 6.3.2(b), we assumed that the sequencing of the pictures depended in a simple way on the effective exchange of information. It was therefore enough just to identify which picture was being described. Let us say now that groups of students have to discover the sequence themselves by working out how the pictures can be combined to form a coherent story. In addition to using the language related to the pictures, they therefore have to negotiate the problem-solving element. This aspect of the task depends on each student's active contribution and cannot be predicted.

When there is a problem to be solved, we can often dispense with the need to distribute the initial information amongst different students, because the problem itself creates a communicative purpose. In place of the 'information gap' that motivates the exchange of simple information, the students need to overcome what is sometimes called an 'opinion gap' (Rixon, 1979) or 'problem-solving gap' (Prabhu, 1987). A familiar example is the so-called 'balloon game', in which students must discuss which of a number of people or objects have to be sacrificed in order to enable the balloon to carry the others safely.

Problem-solving is one of many forms of discussion and I will therefore extend this component to include all forms of classroom discussion as a means for language learning. There is no need here to expand on the variety of ways in which discussion can be stimulated and organized (on this see for example Klippel, 1984; Pattison, 1987; Ur, 1981). However, I would like to emphasize its central importance as a means of using the actual situation of the classroom as a context for learners to express their own meanings in real, creative communication (cf. Rivers, 1987).

6.4.2 Creative role-playing and simulation

In 6.3.3(b) we looked at role-playing tasks as activities in which the meanings that learners express are determined mainly by the teacher or the materials. We have also noted that this control can become gradually looser. The cues can become less detailed and leave more scope for the learners to choose what they want to say. As we move further along the continuum, specific cues can give way to more general information about the situation and the participants' roles and purposes within it (cf. Littlewood, 1981; Livingstone, 1983). As this happens, students enjoy more scope to interact through personal meanings of their own and to become personally involved in the communication that takes place. Gradually, then, they become more able to integrate their own identities with the meanings which grow out of the simulated context and which the language expresses.

The concept of 'role' is a useful one because it can link what takes place in the classroom with what takes place outside it (see for example Littlewood, 1987). It is not only in the classroom that we perform roles. We are doing so all the time in our daily life: in our jobs we perform the role of teacher, perhaps also supervisor or head of department; at home we may perform the role of parent, daughter or son; in other contexts we may perform the role of acquaintance, stranger, novice or expert; and so on. In each context, we normally adapt how we behave in ways that we have learnt to associate with our role. This does not mean that we are not 'being ourselves' in these situations but that the ways we act, even 'as ourselves', are influenced by the kinds of expectations and responsibilities that are attached to particular roles in society (cf. Berger and Luckmann, 1967; Hampson, 1988). There are, of course, some important differences between performing roles inside and outside the classroom. In particular, outside the classroom the social sanctions for *not* adopting the conventional behaviour are more serious than inside. None the less, they share the common feature that in each case it is a matter of adopting behaviour-patterns which originate from outside ourselves. Provided that the learners are able to identify with the roles assigned to them, role-playing therefore provides opportunities for students to climb into the kinds of linguistic behaviour-patterns which they will need to produce outside the classroom and to integrate these behaviour-patterns with their own personalities (cf. Littlewood, 1983).

An activity closely related to role-playing is simulation (cf. Jones, 1982). This term usually refers to an activity in which some kind of problematic *situation* is simulated but, within the situation, the learners are not asked to pretend to be somebody else but simply to act as themselves. For example, they may have to act in the capacity of teachers, parents and governors of a school and decide how to spend a sum of money in order to obtain the most benefit. The difference between 'being oneself' (but in an unfamiliar role) and 'pretending to be somebody else' is not at all clear-cut, of course, but in general, the emphasis in a simulation is on coping with the situation rather than on adopting behaviour-patterns which might be unfamiliar. So far as the learners are concerned, the decisive factor in all these activities is the degree to which they are able to act creatively in their role and integrate the new language with their own identity.

6.4.3   Experiential learning

A logical step forwards from *simulating* situations in which learners have to use language is to *create* these situations from the resources that are actually present in the classroom and (if possible) from those outside it. The students can then develop their language skills not by artificially determined means but by engaging in real experiences which require these skills. This is comparable to how infants develop their first language skills through their direct involvement in experiences.

An obvious but often neglected context for experiential learning is the actual moment-by-moment management of the students' learning experiences in the classroom. In the more traditional, teacher-dominated classroom, the organization of learning revolves mainly around instructions and questions from the teacher, providing only a limited range of opportunities for communication. However, one result of the expanding repertoire of activity-types and the emphasis on learner-centred classrooms in recent years has been that the roles performed by teachers and learners are now far more diverse than previously (cf. Wright, 1987). This means that the organization of learning involves more discussion and negotiation, so that the classroom can become a rich language-environment in its own right. Willis (1981) sets out to prepare non-native teachers for this task and some published courses prepare learners systematically to cope with the everyday communication-needs that arise in the classroom.

The extension of using language to organize learning experiences is to structure the experiences themselves so that they involve the learners in natural language-use. As we saw in section 6.4.1, this takes place in discussion and problem-solving, where learners are faced simply with a topic or problem which they deal with as a 'one-off' task. It takes place within a more extended framework when the learners embark on larger-scale projects involving language. The project provides a global context which motivates a wide variety of specific contexts for natural language-use (reading, discussion in groups, interviewing individuals, presenting results verbally or in writing, and so on). For example, in a project carried out recently at the Bell School in Bath, the learners set out to organize a jumble sale and create a videotape about their experiences. This involved them in reading a large variety of documents, discussing strategies, approaching official authorities, writing letters, preparing posters, presenting the video, and so on. As a further example, the project 'Airport' in Germany (Legutke and Thiel, 1982) involved learners in preparing interview sheets, interviewing travellers at Frankfurt Airport, presenting and writing reports, and so on. Other project topics need not rely on the immediate availability of native speakers (cf. Fried-Booth, 1986; Nunan, 1989). However, as Strevens (1987) points out, it is often possible to find individual native speakers who are happy to be approached.

Under 'experiential learning' we can also include smaller-scale tasks in which the learners have to use the language for learning about some other topic, e.g. through one of the topic-based modules discussed by Allen and Howard (1981).

6.5 Conclusion

We have now added a number of 'whole-task' components to our framework. They all come under the general heading of 'using language for authentic communication' (since this is the goal that we are concerned with here). If we add them to the part-skill activities presented diagrammatically in figure 6.2 we have built up the framework first presented in figure 6.1 above: see figure 6.3.

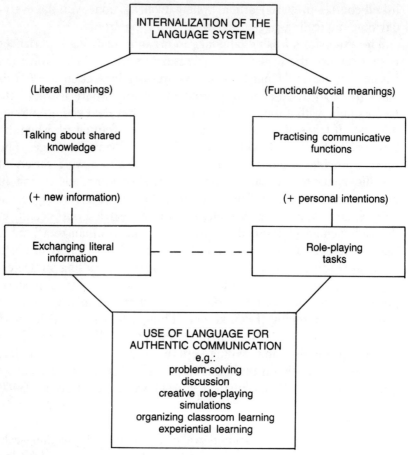

Figure 6.3

In conclusion I would like to repeat that the framework is not intended as a prescription for classroom methodology. Rather, it is a 'conceptual map' to represent how activities relate to each other and to the goals of language teaching.

Nor, therefore, is the framework intended to represent a sequence of activity-types that we should always follow in the classroom. Often our teaching sequences may begin with part-skill practice and lead towards whole-task practice, but this is by no means a necessary procedure. It is equally possible to start a sequence with some form of communication activity. If this reveals gaps in the students' knowledge, these can be remedied through structure-oriented activities, followed by an activity in which the students use the language to exchange information and, perhaps, by another more structure-oriented activity in which they explore the possibilities of the system in more detail (cf. Brumfit, 1984; Littlewood, 1981). Other kinds of sequence emerge naturally from particular classroom situations.

7 Involving the Learners

7.1 Introduction

Chapter 6 described a methodological framework which relates the various procedures for developing oral skills to (a) the learners' goal of communicative ability and (b) different kinds of learning. Since the aim was to draw up a kind of 'conceptual map' by means of which we can orient our activity in the classroom, the main focus was on the structure and content of the methodology.

This chapter shifts the perspective onto the even more fundamental question of how, within this framework or indeed any other we might adopt, we can aim to involve the main actors in the classroom – the learners – in what is taking place. Unless we succeed in this aim, all our other deliberations are largely irrelevant. I will consider four principles which derive partly from discussions in previous chapters and partly from other insights into the conditions for learning:

1 The classroom atmosphere must be conducive to communication and learning.
2 Learning must be relevant to learners' interests and needs.
3 Processes as well as products are important in the language classroom.
4 Learners must perform active roles in the classroom.

7.2   The Classroom Atmosphere must be Conducive to Communication and Learning

The most important condition for learning is that the learners should be ready to engage themselves without constraint in the activities and interactions which take place in their classroom environment. They have to be induced to give up willingly the security of their mother tongue and to accept the 'frustrations of non-communication' and 'initial intellectual and emotional shock' (Stern, 1983: 398) which accompany the first stages of language learning. It is therefore important that the environment should be one which enables them to feel sufficiently secure to make this leap into the unknown.

Over recent years a lot of attention has been paid to the importance of learners' feelings (their 'affective state') in determining the quality of learning that takes place in the classroom. Much of the initial impetus came from trends in education outside language teaching. Humanistic psychologists such as Carl Rogers (1969) emphasized the importance of the 'whole learner' in education and the same message was introduced into language teaching by Curran (1976) and others. They stressed that learners are not simply processors of information who, when they enter the classroom, leave the deeper layers of their identity outside: they are real people who bring with them a whole array of personal attributes and feelings. These have to be respected, if individual development and growth are to take place. One of the fundamental tasks of the teacher as a facilitator of learning is therefore to 'make space for the learner' in the classroom (cf. Spaventa, 1980).

A first step towards making space for the learner is to reduce the dominance of the teacher. This is obviously related to the need for learners to perform active roles (cf. section 7.5). However it is not only a question of assigning more active roles. It would be possible to do this in a threatening spirit and make learners feel that their new responsibility is more likely to lead them to fail than to succeed. Active roles can only be exercised creatively if the learners also feel that there is no threat to their egos (which are so openly exposed in the foreign-language classroom) from a critical and unaccepting audience. The teacher must signal, through his or her way of acting and being, that the classroom is a human environment in which all members are listened to positively and accepted as co-contributors to the events. This is partly a matter of how these events are organized but, even more, it depends on the quality of the interpersonal interaction which the teacher is able to stimulate.

Equally important as the relationship between teacher and learners is, of course, the relationship between the learners themselves. Ideally the class should provide a network of human relationships in which all learners feel accepted, supported and encouraged by each other. Clearly the attitude of the teacher, mentioned above, is one crucial factor in encouraging this kind of interpersonal climate to grow amongst learners. Another is the nature of the communication patterns that emerge from the activities in which the learners are involved. The current acceptance of pair- and group-work as a major mode of working opens up opportunities for interaction between learners that are not present in the more formal, 'lockstep' pattern of teaching (cf. Wright, 1987). Learners can cooperate in the joint solution of tasks and thus form a learning community to which everybody contributes. They can get to know each other as individuals and determine together the nature of the human environment in which they work. One of the most satisfying features of an activity carried out in groups or pairs is to see how each group settles into its own preferred style of interacting: some pursue their aims with quiet seriousness, some with lightness and humour, and so on. Although the teacher may have organized the structures within which the interactions take place, it is the learners themselves who create the interactions.

'Making space for the learners' means that each individual learner should not feel threatened by forces outside his or her control (e.g. a negatively-disposed audience) and should not feel that his or her social identity is submerged anonymously within the class. When these conditions exist, they also make possible a further aspect of the involvement of the whole person in the learning process: that learners should have opportunities to express their own identities. One way of achieving this is through the active roles mentioned in section 7.5 below: whenever learners make a choice between alternative meanings, roles or activities, they are expressing their own identities indirectly. More direct forms of self-expression can occur when we relate the content of an activity to the learners' own circumstances, e.g. in the course of a discussion or through techniques for 'personalizing' language practice (cf. Harmer, 1983: 95–8).

Opportunities for self-expression such as those just described demand comparatively little overt exposure of the individual's feelings and, as such, are likely to be acceptable to all learners. Beyond this, however, we need also to remember that many people do not enjoy talking openly about themselves and that in many cultures it is considered inappropriate to do so (cf. Valdes, 1987). Providing opportunities for self-expression should therefore not be confused with organizing activities in which learners are compelled to talk about matters which they regard as personal (cf. Brumfit, 1982; Stevick, 1990). For many groups, the more self-revelatory forms of communication such as those required by some 'humanistic' techniques (cf. Moskowitz, 1978) will prove inappropriate. This is a domain in which it is important for the teacher to be sensitive to the preferences and needs of each specific group of learners.

In the past, one of the main obstacles to creating the kind of atmosphere in which the emphasis is on acceptance rather than rejection has been the obligation that we have felt to focus on the area in which learners are most deficient; namely, accurate control of the language system. This has sometimes led to an almost continuous focus on learners' errors rather than their successes and has often engendered a sense of inadequacy and hopelessness, particularly amongst slower learners. The present emphasis on the process of communicating rather than on the accuracy of the language produced (cf. section 7.4) enables us to reverse this trend. Although error-correction still has its place, it is no longer the main form of feedback. Errors take their place amongst many other aspects of the language learner's performance, which can be evaluated (in class as well as in testing) more for its positive aspects than for its shortcomings (cf. Hughes, 1989; Lee, 1989; Underhill, 1987). This enables us to focus attention firmly on what learners can *achieve* rather than what they lack, with beneficial effects both for individual learners' self-esteem and for the classroom atmosphere.

7.3 Learning must be Relevant to Learners' Interests and Needs

It is a fundamental characteristic of teaching that whereas we can create *contexts which facilitate* learning, we have no direct control over the *actual processes* of learning. These depend on the learners themselves. One important factor in encouraging learning to take place was considered in section 7.2: that the classroom environment should be conducive to learning and communication. Another important factor is that the learners must feel motivated to engage with the specific experiences and materials which we offer them.

At a general level, the importance of motivation as a factor leading to success in language learning is well established. A common distinction is often drawn between an 'integrative' orientation to learning and an 'instrumental' orientation (cf. Gardner, 1985; Skehan, 1989). Students whose motivation is predominantly integrative want to learn the language in order to communicate with native speakers of the language. Those whose motivation is primarily instrumental want to learn the language for some other, more extrinsic reason (for example, to pass an examination or gain social advancement). This does not mean that learners fall neatly into one category or the other: the motivation of any specific individual is likely to be a subtle mixture of the two motives. For example, the underlying reason for wanting to communicate with native speakers (an 'integrative' motive) may be partly to improve one's employment prospects (an 'instrumental' motive). Alternatively, a person whose initial desire is only to pass an examination may become increasingly attracted by the language itself and the people who speak it. In most studies, the integrative motive has been found to produce the best learning. This is not surprising, since it is more likely to reflect a true desire to engage in regular, moment-by-moment contact with the language and its speakers.

In the classroom, this moment-by-moment involvement depends partly on the students' initial motivation but even more on whether the actual learning experiences seem relevant to their interests and needs. Relevance is not such a simple notion as it appears at first sight, however. We need to keep more than one kind in mind.

The simplest and most obvious kind of relevance is related to language use outside the classroom. It depends on whether the students are able to connect what they are learning with what they will need for their future foreign-language roles. The search for this kind of relevance is one of the main justifications for syllabuses based on communicative categories such as functions or notions: if learners are involved in practising 'how to ask for things in shops' or 'how to introduce themselves', they can see right from the start that their learning has 'pay-off' value in terms of everyday communicative needs (cf. Wilkins, 1976; Johnson, 1982). This first kind of relevance is also one of the reasons for using so-called 'authentic materials' such as menus or brochures (cf. Aplin, 1989; Little et al., 1988) and involving learners in 'authentic tasks' such as writing letters or listening to announcements (cf. Fowler, 1989; Jones, 1989). When we look for this kind of relevance, we emphasize the fact that the classroom's function is to prepare learners for situations in the outside world and measure how closely our classroom activities mirror those outside.

The kind of relevance just described has obvious superficial validity for most learners. On its own, however, it often has little power to grip their imagination and, if it is the sole focus of the course, can quickly lose their interest. To spend all one's time pretending to book rooms in hotels that do not exist, reading menus for meals one will never eat and listening for the times of trains one will never take, can be no less stultifying than the long dictations that we often had to write in the past. We therefore have to strive to achieve a second kind of relevance, which appeals to the deeper interests and concerns of the learners as individuals: a sense that language is a living medium through which they can interact with each other as human beings and express meanings that are important to them. This kind of relevance depends not so much on the extent to which the classroom is a substitute for the outside world as on its value as a meaningful social context in its own right (cf. Breen, 1985; Kramsch, 1987). In order to achieve it, the most important factor is not whether the materials and activities are authentic in comparison with those outside the classroom: it is whether the learners' *response* is authentic, in the sense of being rooted in their own personalities and growing out of the immediate interaction between participants in the real classroom situation (cf. Widdowson, 1979, 1990).

Our first priority in the classroom has to be that the learners' experiences there should enable them to engage their minds with the language and thus internalize its resources in such a way that they can later deploy them creatively in different contexts (cf. Prabhu, 1987). It is therefore the second kind of relevance and authenticity that is most crucial. For some learners, the first kind may be a necessary condition in order to create confidence in the value of their learning and, as a result, a frame of mind in which the second, more personal kind of relevance can grow. For other learners, on the other hand, the strongest degree of mind-engagement may occur through experiences of, say, an imaginative or aesthetic nature, which bear little superficial resemblance to the situations where they will later use the language. The language competence which these experiences allow to develop can be transferred, either later or as a parallel strand within the course, to more everyday situations such as booking rooms or asking directions.

In the same way, in mother-tongue development, the language which we have acquired initially through the interpersonal and imaginative experiences of childhood can later be deployed in the completely different range of situations that make up adult life.

7.4 Processes as well as Products are Important in the Language Classroom

In chapters 1 and 2 we saw that communication is a process in which people 'do things with words' as they participate in social interaction. So long as the participants in a conversation continue to share meanings with each other and respond in unpredictable ways, this process is in a state of constant movement. Many of its most important aspects are also invisible, since the speakers' intended meanings and mental responses lie beneath the surface of what can be seen and heard. For both of these reasons, the process cannot be recaptured after the event and it cannot be observed. All that we can observe are its products: the words that are spoken (particularly if these are recorded) and any tangible outcome of the communication, such as a written report or agreement. However, even these products have a different significance afterwards, since they are divorced from the situational and interpersonal context which contributed to their original meaning. Thus we can argue endlessly about 'what somebody meant' by a particular set of words but the argument can never be finally resolved, because the moment and context of the utterance can never be recreated.

In spite of the fact that we are primarily interested, in language teaching, in developing the learners' ability to take part in the process of communication, we tend to focus a lot of attention on observable products. We do this in two main ways. First, we are often most happy when the students are involved in producing some kind of tangible outcome that can be evaluated: a completed exercise, an essay or a written dialogue. In the context of the classroom, indeed, we often come to regard this outcome as more important than the creative processes that produce it. Second, we often find ourselves devoting more attention to the forms of the language that the learners produce – in particular, their formal accuracy – than to their effectiveness in enabling communication to take place.

As a pedagogical technique, the setting of tasks which demand some tangible outcome is well established. In many situations, it is the most effective way of motivating the learners and orienting their language activity: in order to create a tangible product, they engage those internal processes of communication and learning which they need to develop. Ur (1981) makes this point in relation to discussions and it underlies the current interest in task-based learning (cf. Nunan, 1989). However, even though the need to produce a concrete outcome may dominate the learners' (perhaps also the teacher's) attention while the activity is in progress, the activity must derive its ultimate methodological justification not from the quality of this outcome but from the quality of the language activity that produces it. For example, although Prabhu (1987) intends his problem-solving tasks to provide the sole focus for the teacher's and learners' attention in the classroom, we are ultimately interested not in whether the learners find the right answers but in whether their attempts to find them stimulate useful communication and learning-processes. Only if this is the case are they justified in methodological terms. The same is true of more traditional learning activities such as dictation or writing dialogues. When we ask students to collaborate in writing a dialogue, for example, we hope that the work which they invest into arriving at an agreed version will engage their learning capacities with the foreign language in useful ways. Once the final product exists, it has fulfilled its purpose and becomes unimportant.

At this point, however, we must begin to make provisos. In the context of the learners' *overall development*, the products that emerge from activities are less important than the processes they have stimulated. In the *immediate classroom context*, however, these processes are most likely to be stimulated when the learners attach importance to the products they have been asked to create. It is when they are most keenly motivated to find the best solutions to problems, write the most interesting dialogues or produce the most attractive projects, that they are most likely to engage intensively in learning and communication. Thus, the most beneficial effects on processes are likely to result from affirming the value of the products. Likewise, the quality of the product is one indicator of the quality of the processes that created it and often – for example, in the case of reports or letters – the main yardstick by which success is measured. There is thus a delicate balance in language teaching between focusing on products and focusing on processes.

This delicate balance is also evident when we come to consider the issues of formal accuracy and the correction of errors. Communication is a process of conveying meanings and our main aim in language teaching is to enable learners to take part in this process. In this respect, when they communicate in the classroom, it does not matter whether the linguistic products of this process – the words we can hear – are formally correct, so long as they enable the intended meanings to be conveyed in that particular situation. Correction of errors would appear to be not only inappropriate to the purposes of using language but also likely to distract the learners' attention from the all-important level of meaning. This attitude is reflected, in testing, in the way that credit is now usually given for conveying meanings irrespective of the accuracy of the language produced (which is generally, however, evaluated as a separate dimension – cf. Lee, 1989) and, in classroom methodology, in the way that teachers often withhold error-correction during meaning-focused activities (or, in the terminology of Brumfit, 1984, 'fluency activities').

Again, however, we must make provisos. In the language classroom we are not only interested in the communication that is currently in progress. We are interested in equipping learners with a sufficient degree of control over grammar and vocabulary to enable them also to convey meanings clearly in *future* situations, including situations where the complexity of the messages might demand more accurate control over grammatical and lexical distinctions. We are therefore compelled to look beyond the immediate communication and focus on its linguistic products, in order to develop the language system that the learners have at their disposal. In some cases this may involve the teacher noting formal errors for future treatment, in order to avoid interrupting the activity while it is in progress. In other cases, notably in more form-oriented ('part-skill') activities, it may be more appropriate to provide immediate correction. The focus has thus to be finely balanced between communicative process and linguistic product, in ways that aim not only to support the learners' capacity to become involved in the immediate communication but also to equip them with a more polished instrument for future use.

When we require concrete outcomes from task-based learning activities, then, we are focusing on products primarily for the sake of the processes that produce them. Once they have been produced, their purpose has been served. When we correct the language forms that learners produce, the opposite is the case: we are focusing on the products of the activity because of their potential importance in the future.

7.5 Learners must Perform Active Roles in the Classroom

When learning was believed to be a simple matter of habit-formation, the role of language learners was seen as correspondingly passive. Infants were regarded as 'blank slates' onto which first-language habits were engraved. Foreign-language learners needed to have these habits changed through controlled repetition and drilling of new forms. In each case the active stimuli for learning were to be found outside the learner.

We saw in chapters 3 and 4 that, whether we regard language learning as skill-learning or natural growth, the emphasis has now shifted onto the active roles that learners themselves must play. Both the internalization of cognitive skills through conscious learning and the creative construction of a mental system through subconscious acquisition depend crucially on the active processing that is carried out by the learners themselves. This depends, in its turn, on the learners' active involvement in shaping their own interaction with and through the language. This emphasis on active learner involvement lies at the heart of 'learner-centred' approaches to foreign-language teaching (cf. Burton, 1987; Dickinson, 1987; Little, 1991; Nunan 1988).

Adopting active roles implies that the learners make choices and decisions which affect their own learning activity. These choices can vary widely in their scope and complexity, however, and teachers can manipulate this variation in order to ensure that the choices suit the capability of the learners and nature of the activity. Since using a language involves making choices in any case, it is largely a question of extending these choices further up a scale so that, as their course progresses, learners become more and more capable of operating independently both in their communication and in their learning.

At the lowest end of the scale of learner-choices, it is still the teacher who determines what activity the learners should perform and what their roles should be within it. Within these roles, however, the learners themselves have control over the interaction and the information. Once the activity is in progress, the teacher does not intervene unless the interaction cannot proceed without help. This simple kind of learner-centredness is a characteristic of a large number of the group- and pair-work activities, such as role-playing and information-exchange tasks, which now perform a major role in our methodology for developing communication skills (cf. chapter 6 and, for example, Byrne, 1986, 1987). The learners have to make a lot of choices, and these can demand varying degrees of skill and creativity, but they affect only the ongoing interaction and do not have consequences outside it. The teacher retains overall control of the content of the activities and progression of the course.

As we move further along the scale, the scope of the learners' choices widens. A significant stage is reached when, even though the task itself is still determined by the teacher, the learners have greater freedom to shape for themselves the roles they will adopt within it. More creative kinds of role-playing or improvisation enable this kind of freedom (cf. Littlewood, 1981: ch. 5), as also do discussions and debates in which the students must decide their own attitude or argument with respect to the issue under discussion (cf. Ur, 1981). The teacher's role is now to construct a looser kind of framework which the learners themselves can fill with their own ideas and personalities.

As this teacher-controlled framework becomes looser, the scope of the learners' choices continues to widen. Another significant stage is reached when the learners are free to choose the actual tasks which they will perform. In project-based activities, for example, a group of students may be assigned a topic by the teacher but be free to distribute amongst themselves the various sub-tasks that the pro-ject involves, such as reading brochures, interviewing native-speak-ers, and so on (cf. Fried-Booth, 1986). On another occasion they may be asked to decide for themselves on the topic and the most appropriate way of dividing the work into sub-tasks. Reducing the degree of control still further, Dam (1988) describes a learner-centred approach in which groups of learners are free to choose for themselves, in consultation with the teacher, what learning activities they wish to carry out and what outcomes they want to produce. Self-access systems (Little, 1989) require a similar degree of learner choice.

The adoption of active roles by the learners presupposes that they are ready (i.e. both willing and able) to take on responsibility for making the choices involved. There is an abundance of anecdotal accounts of the chaos that can result when a teacher gives learners a greater degree of freedom than they are so far able to cope with. This readiness to accept responsibility has three main aspects, each of which the teacher can aim to develop by gradual stages. The first is a matter of how learners perceive their own roles in the classroom. Learners who are accustomed to seeing the teacher's role as to choose and dictate, while their own role is to accept and follow, may resist an attempt to change this balance and even perceive the teacher as weak or incompetent (cf. Wright, 1987). In this case the teacher will need to re-shape the role-relationship gradually, beginning by asking the learners to make small choices within an otherwise controlled framework. The second aspect concerns the knowledge and skills that are required in order to exercise choices. It is meaningless, for example, to ask learners to express preferences about learning activities when they know nothing about the alternatives. At any particular stage, then, any alternatives presented to the learners must be of kinds which are familiar to them. Similarly, before asking learners to interact independently, the teacher must ensure that they have the necessary knowledge and skills to cope not only with the language but also with the task that has been assigned. The third aspect is whether the learners have sufficient confidence in themselves. In the traditional teacher-dominated classroom, the typical exchange pattern is 'teacher initiates → learner responds → teacher evaluates' (cf. Coulthard, 1983). This pattern demands little initiative from the learners and protects them from the need to make any but the lowest-level choices. If they are asked too suddenly to operate outside this tight framework, they can feel inadequate and insecure. Again, then, their confidence needs to be nurtured gradually. The teacher needs to increase gradually the level of the choices which they are required to make, so that they never feel they have been thrown into an unstructured environment without enough support to survive.

This emphasis on active roles for learners can be justified not only in terms of the demands of the learning process and of the independent use they must later make of the language. It is also related to the learners' broader personal development. As they become able to accept more active roles in the social context of the classroom, they will also become better able to take responsibility for organizing their own learning in later life and to develop greater autonomy as individuals in other situations of life (cf. Holec, 1981; Little, 1991; Van Ek, 1986).

7.6   Conclusion

The paramount importance of involving the learners in what goes on in the classroom seems now to be self-evident. To good teachers, it probably always has been. It is comparatively recently, however, that this need has been explicitly recognized in discussions about methodology, where the assumption has mainly been that the learners will simply follow directions determined by the teacher and the method. When a book appeared in 1973 with the title *Focus on the Learner* (Oller and Richards), the very choice of title indicated that this was for many people an unfamiliar perspective: hitherto, the focus had been mainly on language and the teacher.

It is now part of our basic assumptions in language teaching that we have to start from where the learners are rather than from some point outside them. The yardstick by which we must judge any new idea or technique is not whether it corresponds to an abstract principle of linguistics, psychology or methodology, but whether it stimulates purposeful and useful learning in a specific group of learners. Since learners differ so widely from each other in how they respond, 'focusing on the learners' is now an essential activity not only for researchers but also for teachers (cf. Allwright, 1988).

Conclusion

This book has attempted to straddle the borderline between theory and practice and explore how they can be linked to form a coherent approach to teaching oral communication in the classroom. It began by considering those elements of present-day theories of language and learning which seem most relevant to a teacher's search for a suitable methodology. It then presented a methodological framework which could accommodate these various elements into a blueprint for teaching, which could orient us in our teaching but retain enough flexibility to be adapted to different situations. At the end, after the discussion had moved through language, learning and teaching, it returned to the most important factor to be considered in teaching: the learners themselves, their roles in the classroom, and how we can involve them in what we offer.

Because the book has tried to keep one foot in theory and one in practice, it is inevitable that there has not been space to deal exhaustively with either. That is the main reason why, in the course of the book, I have taken care to refer to other books and articles which are suitable to take the reader further in either direction. The reader who is interested in setting off on a more intensive exploration of theory could profitably move now – if he or she has not already done so – to the work of Stern (1983), which is outstanding in the breadth and accessibility of its treatment of the 'fundamental concepts' on which language teaching is based. The reader who wishes to embark on a more detailed examination of the practical implications of adopting a 'communicative' approach could move to the work of Harmer (1983), which provides excellent coverage of the repertoire of activities that now exists for developing not only oral skills but also those of reading and writing. On the continuum from theory to practice, I would like to see the present book as lying between the two just mentioned.

So much has taken place in language study and language teaching in recent years that the journey in either direction cannot be other than full of fascination and variety.

References

Abbs, B., and Freebairn, I. (1977) *Starting Strategies*, London: Longman.

Allen, J. P. B., and Howard, J. (1981) 'Subject-related ESL: an experiment in communicative language teaching', *Canadian Modern Language Review*, 37: 535–50.

Allwright, R. L. (1988) *Observation in the Language Classroom*, London: Longman.

Anderson, J. R. (1985) *Cognitive Psychology and its Implications*, 2nd ed. New York: W. H. Freeman and Co.

Aplin, R. (1989) 'Using authentic materials for GCSE' in Littlewood, W. T., (ed.), *Developing Modern Language Skills for GCSE*. Walton-on-Thames: Nelson.

Argyle, M. (1978) *The Psychology of Interpersonal Behaviour*, 3rd ed. Harmondsworth: Penguin Books.

Austin, J. L. (1962) *How To Do Things With Words*. Oxford: Clarendon Press.

Beattie, G. (1983) *Talk: An Analysis of Speech and Non-Verbal Behaviour in Conversation*. Milton Keynes: Open University Press.

Berger, P. L., and Luckmann, T. (1967) *The Social Construction of Reality*. Harmondsworth: Penguin Books.

Bialystock, E. (1990) *Communication Strategies*. Oxford: Basil Blackwell.

Bird, E., and Dennison, M. (1987) *Teaching GCSE Modern Languages*. London: Hodder and Stoughton.

Bowers, R. G., Bamber, B., Straker Cook, R., and Thomas, A. L. (1987) *Talking about Grammar*. London: Longman.

Breen, M. P. (1985) 'Authenticity in the language classroom'. *Applied Linguistics*, 6: 60–70.

Brooks, N. (1960) *Language and Language Learning*. New York: Harcourt Brace and World.

Brown, H. D. (1980) *Principles of Language Learning and Teaching*. Englewood Cliffs, NJ: Prentice Hall.

Brown, P., and Levinson, S. (1978) 'Universals in language usage: politeness phenomena' in Goody, E. N. (ed.), *Questions and Politeness: Strategies in Social Interaction*. Cambridge: Cambridge University Press.

Brown, R. (1973) *A First Language: The Early Stages*. Harmondsworth: Penguin Books.

Brumfit, C. J. (1982) 'Some humanistic doubts about humanistic language teaching' in Early, P. (ed.), *Humanistic Approaches: An Empirical View*. London: British Council.

Brumfit, C. J. (1984) *Communicative Methodology in Language Teaching*. Cambridge: Cambridge University Press.

Bruner, J. S. (1975) 'The ontogenesis of speech acts'. *Journal of Child Language*, 2: 1–19.

Bruner, J. S., and Haste, H. W. (eds) (1987) *Making Sense*. London: Methuen.

Buckby, M. (1989) 'Developing speaking skills for GCSE' in Littlewood, W. T. (ed.) *Developing Modern Language Skills for GCSE*. Walton-on-Thames: Nelson.

Burton, J. (ed.) (1987) *Implementing the Learner-Centred Curriculum*. Adelaide: National Curriculum Resource Centre.

Byrne, D. (1986) *Teaching Oral English*, 2nd ed. London: Longman.

Byrne, D. (1987) *Techniques for Oral Interaction*. London: Longman.

Canale, M. (1983) 'From communicative competence to communicative language pedagogy' in Richards, J. C., and Schmidt, R. (eds), *Language and Communication*. London: Longman.

Carroll, J. B. (1971) 'Current issues in psycholinguistics and second language teaching', *TESOL Quarterly*, 5: 101–14.

Cook. V. J. (1982) 'Structure drills and the language learner'. *Canadian Modern Language Review*, 38: 321–9.

Cook. V. J. (1991) *Second Language Learning and Language Teaching*. London: Edward Arnold.

Corder, S. P. (1981) *Error Analysis and Interlanguage*. Oxford: Oxford University Press.

Coulthard, M. (1983) *An Introduction to Discourse Analysis*, 2nd ed. London: Longman.

Crystal, D. (1986) *Listen to Your Child: A Parents' Guide to Children's Language*. Harmondsworth: Penguin Books.

Curran, C. (1976) *Counselling-Learning in Second Languages*. Apple River, Ill.: Apple River Press.

Dakin, J. (1973) *The Language Laboratory and Language Learning*. London: Longman.

Dam, L. (1988) 'Developing autonomy in schools: why and how', *Language Teacher*, 1: 22–33.

Davies, P., Roberts, J., and Rossner, R. (1975) *Situational Lesson Plans*. London: Macmillan.

de Villiers, P. A., and de Villiers, J. G. (1979) *Early Language*. London: Fontana and Open Books.

Dickinson, L. (1987) *Self-Instruction in Language Learning*. Cambridge: Cambridge University Press.

Diller, K. C. (1978) *The Language Teaching Controversy*. Rowley, Mass.: Newbury House.

Edmondson, W., and House, J. (1981) *Let's Talk and Talk about It: A Pedagogic Interactional Grammar of English*. Munich: Urban and Schwarzenberg.

Ellis, A. W., and Beattie, G. (1986) *The Psychology of Language and Communication*. London: Weidenfeld and Nicolson.

Ellis, R. (1985) *Understanding Second Language Acquisition*. Oxford: Oxford University Press.

Faerch, C., and Kasper, G. (eds) (1983) *Strategies in Interlanguage Communication*. London: Longman.

Felix, S. W. (1981) 'The effect of formal instruction on second language acquisition'. *Language Learning*, 31: 87–112.

Fowler, M. (1989) 'Developing writing skills' in Littlewood, W. T. (ed.), *Developing Modern Language Skills for GCSE*. Walton-on-Thames: Nelson.

Fried-Booth, D. L. (1986) *Project Work*. Oxford: Oxford University Press.

Gardner, R. C. (1985) *Social Psychology and Second Language Learning*. London: Edward Arnold.

Garrett, M. F. (1982) 'Production of speech: observations from normal and pathological language use', in Ellis, A. W. (ed.), *Normality and Pathology in Cognitive Functions*. London: Academic Press.

Graddol, D., Cheshire, J., and Swann, J. (1987) *Describing Language*. Milton Keynes: Open University Press.

Gregg, K. (1984) 'Krashen's Monitor and Occam's Razor'. *Applied Linguistics*, 5: 79–100.

Halliday, M. A. K. (1975) *Learning How to Mean*. London: Edward Arnold.

Halliday, M. A. K. (1985) *An Introduction to Functional Grammar*. London: Edward Arnold.

Halliday, M. A. K. (1987) 'Language and the order of nature' in Fabb, N., Attridge, D., Durant, A. and MacCabe, C. (eds), *The Linguistics of Writing*. Manchester: Manchester University Press.

Hampson, S. E. (1988) *The Construction of Personality*, 2nd ed. London: Routledge.

Harley, B., and Swain, M. (1984) 'The interlanguage of immersion students and its implications for second language learning' in Davies, A., Criper, C., and Howatt, A. P. R. (eds), *Interlanguage*. Edinburgh: Edinburgh University Press.

Harmer, J. (1983) *The Practice of English Language Teaching*. Oxford: Oxford University Press.

Harmer, J. (1987) *Teaching and Learning Grammar*. London: Longman.

Harris, M., and Coltheart, M. (1990) *Language Processing in Children and Adults*. London: Routledge.

Hatch, E. M. (ed.) (1978) *Second Language Acquisition: A Book of Readings*, Rowley, Mass.: Newbury House.

Holec, H. (1981) *Autonomy in Foreign Language Learning*. Oxford: Pergamon Press.

Howatt, A. P. R. (1984) *A History of English Language Teaching*. Oxford: Oxford University Press.

Hubbard, P., Jones, H., Thornton, B., and Wheeler, R. (1983) *A Training Course for TEFL*. Oxford: Oxford University Press.

Hughes, A. (1989) *Testing for Language Teachers*. Cambridge: Cambridge University Press.

James, C. (1983) 'A two-stage approach to language teaching' in Johnson, K., and Porter, D. (eds), *Perspectives in Communicative Language Teaching*. London: Academic Press.

Johnson, K. (1982) *Communicative Syllabus Design and Methodology*. Oxford: Pergamon Press.

Johnson, K., and Morrow, K. (eds) (1981) *Communication in the Classroom*. London: Longman.

Jones, B. (1989) 'Listening' in Littlewood, W. T. (ed.), *Developing Modern Language Skills for GCSE*. Walton-on-Thames: Nelson.

Jones, K. (1982) *Simulations in Language Teaching*. Cambridge: Cambridge University Press.

Klippel, F. (1984) *Keep Talking*, Cambridge: Cambridge University Press.

Kramsch, C. J. (1987) 'Interactive discourse in small and large groups' in Rivers, W. M. (ed.), *Interactive Language Teaching*. Cambridge: Cambridge University Press.

Krashen, S. D. (1981) *Second Language Acquisition and Second Language Learning*. Oxford: Pergamon Press.

Krashen, S. D. (1982) *Principles and Practice in Second Language Acquisition*, Oxford: Pergamon Press.

Krashen, S. D. (1985) *The Input Hypothesis*. London: Longman.

Krashen, S. D., and Terrell, T. D. (1983) *The Natural Approach: Language Acquisition in the Classroom*. Oxford: Pergamon Press.

Larsen-Freeman, D., and Long, M. H. (eds) (1991) *An Introduction to Second Language Acquisition Research*. London: Longman.

Larson, D. N., and Smalley, W. A. (1972) *Becoming Bilingual: A Guide to Language Learning*. New Canaan, Conn.: Practical Anthropology.

Lee, B. (1989) 'Assessing writing and speaking skills' in Littlewood, W. T. (ed.), *Developing Modern Language Skills for GCSE*. Walton-on-Thames: Nelson.

Legutke, M., and Thiel, W. (1982) 'AIRPORT – Bericht über ein Projekt im Englischunterricht in Klasse 6'. *Westermanns Pädagogische Beiträge*, 34: 288–99.

Levelt, W. J. M. (1978) 'Skill theory and language teaching'. *Studies in Second Language Acquisition*, 1: 53–70.

Levinson, S. (1983) *Pragmatics*. Cambridge: Cambridge University Press.

Little, D. (ed.) (1989) *Self-Access Systems for Language Learning*. Dublin: Authentik, in association with CILT, London.

Little, D. (1991) *Learner Autonomy: Definitions, Issues and Problems*. Dublin: Authentik.

Little, D., Devitt, S., and Singleton, D. (1988) *Authentic Texts in Foreign Language Teaching: Theory and Practice*. Dublin: Authentik, in association with CILT, London.

Littlewood, W. T. (1981) *Communicative Language Teaching: An Introduction*. Cambridge: Cambridge University Press.

Littlewood, W. T. (1983) 'Contrastive pragmatics and the foreign language learner's personality'. *Applied Linguistics*, 4: 200–6.

Littlewood, W. T, (1984) *Foreign and Second Language Learning.* Cambridge: Cambridge University Press.

Littlewood, W. T. (1987) 'Social and psychological influences on advanced language learning' in Coleman, J. A. and Towell, R. (eds), *The Advanced Language Learner.* London: CILT.

Littlewood, W. T. (ed.) (1989) *Developing Modern Language Skills for GCSE.* Walton-on-Thames: Nelson.

Livingstone, C. (1983) *Role Play in Language Learning.* London: Longman.

Long, M. H. (1985) 'Input and second language acquisition theory' in Gass, S. and Madden, C. (eds), *Input in Second Language Acquisition.* Rowley, Mass.: Newbury House.

Lyons, J. (1981) *Language and Linguistics: An Introduction.* Cambridge: Cambridge University Press.

McLaughlin, B. (1987) *Theories of Second-Language Learning.* London: Edward Arnold.

Maley, A. (1981) 'Games and problem solving' in Johnson, K, and Morrow, K. (eds), *Communication in the Classroom.* London: Longman.

Mitchell-Kernan, C. and Kernan, K. T. (1977) 'Pragmatics of directive choice among children' in Ervin-Tripp, S., and Mitchell-Kernan, C., (eds), *Child Discourse.* New York: Academic Press.

Moskowitz, G. (1978) *Caring and Sharing in the Foreign Language Classroom.* Rowley, Mass.: Newbury House.

Nunan, D. (1988) *The Learner-Centred Curriculum.* Cambridge: Cambridge University Press.

Nunan, D. (1989) *Designing Tasks for the Communicative Classroom.* Cambridge: Cambridge University Press.

Oller, J., and Richards, J. (eds) (1973) *Focus on the Learner.* Rowley, Mass.: Newbury House.

O'Malley, J. M., and Chamot, A. U. (1990) *Learning Strategies in Second Language Acquisition.* Cambridge: Cambridge University Press.

Pattison, P. (1987) *Developing Communication Skills.* Cambridge: Cambridge University Press.

Pienemann, M. (1985) 'Learnability and syllabus construction' in Pienemann, M., and Hyltenstam, H. (eds), *Modelling and Assessing Second Language Acquisition,* Clevedon: Multilingual Matters.

Pienemann, M. (1989) 'Is language teachable?' *Applied Linguistics,* 10: 52–79.

Prabhu, N. S. (1987) *Second Language Pedagogy*. Oxford: Oxford University Press.

Revell, J. (1979) *Teaching Techniques for Communicative English*. London: Macmillan.

Richards, J. C., and Rodgers, T. S. (1986) *Approaches and Methods in Language Teaching*. Cambridge: Cambridge University Press.

Rivers, W. M. (1964) *The Psychologist and the Foreign Language Teacher*. Chicago: University of Chicago Press.

Rivers, W. M. (1975) *A Practical Guide to the Teaching of French*. New York: Oxford University Press.

Rivers, W. M. (1980) 'Foreign language acquisition: where the real problems lie', *Applied Linguistics*, 1: 48–59.

Rivers, W. M. (1981) *Teaching Foreign-Language Skills*, 2nd ed. Chicago: University of Chicago Press.

Rivers. W. M. (1983) *Communicating Naturally in a Second Language*. Cambridge: Cambridge University Press.

Rivers, W. M. (ed.) (1987) *Interactive Language Teaching*. Cambridge: Cambridge University Press.

Rixon, S. (1979) 'The "information gap" and the "opinion gap" – ensuring that communication games are communicative', *English Language Teaching Journal*, 33: 104–6.

Rogers, C. (1969) *Freedom to Learn*. Ohio: Charles E. Merrill.

Sajavaara, K. (1978) 'The monitor model and monitoring in foreign language speech communication' in Gingras, R. C. (ed.) *Second Language Acquisition and Foreign Language Teaching*. Washington, DC: Center for Applied Linguistics.

Schumann, J. (1978) 'Social and psychological factors in second language acquisition' in Richards, J. C. (ed.), *Understanding Second and Foreign Language Learning*. Rowley, Mass.: Newbury House.

Scott, R. (1981) 'Speaking' in Johnson, K., and Morrow, K. (eds), *Communication in the Classroom*. London: Longman.

Sharwood Smith, M. (1981) 'Consciousness raising and the second language learner'. *Applied Linguistics*, 2: 159–68.

Shepherd, J., Rossner, R., and Taylor, J. (1984) *Ways to Grammar: A Modern English Practice Book*. London: Macmillan.

Sinclair, J., and Coulthard, M. (1975) *Towards an Analysis of Discourse*. Oxford: Oxford University Press.

Skehan, P. (1989) *Individual Differences in Second-Language Learning*. London: Edward Arnold.

Smyth, M. M., Morris, P. E., Levy, P., and Ellis, A. W. (1987) *Cognition in Action*. Hove: Lawrence Erlbaum.

Spaventa, L. (ed.) (1980) *Towards the Creative Teaching of English*. London: Allen & Unwin.

Spolsky, B. (1989) *Conditions for Second Language Learning*. Oxford: Oxford University Press.

Stern, H. H. (1983) *Fundamental Concepts of Language Teaching*. Oxford: Oxford University Press.

Stevick, E. W. (1990) *Humanism in Language Teaching*. Oxford: Oxford University Press.

Strevens, P. (1987) 'Interaction outside the classroom: using the community' in Rivers, W. M. (ed.), *Interactive Language Teaching*. Cambridge: Cambridge University Press.

Sturtridge, G. (1981) 'Role-play and simulations' in Johnson, K., and Morrow, K. (eds) *Communication in the Classroom*. London: Longman.

Swain, M. (1985) 'Communicative competence: some roles of comprehensible input and comprehensible output in its development' in Gass, S., and Madden, C. (eds), *Input in Second Language Acquisition*. Rowley, Mass.: Newbury House.

Tarone, E. (1988) *Variation in Interlanguage*. London: Edward Arnold.

Tarone, E., and Yule, G. (1989) *Focus on the Language Learner*. Oxford: Oxford University Press.

Underhill, N. (1987) *Testing Spoken Language*. Cambridge: Cambridge University Press.

Ur, P. (1981) *Discussions that Work*. Cambridge: Cambridge University Press.

Ur, P. (1984) *Teaching Listening Comprehension*. Cambridge: Cambridge University Press.

Ur, P. (1988) *Grammar Practice Activities*. Cambridge: Cambridge University Press.

Valdes, J. M. (ed.) (1987) *Culture Bound*. New York: Cambridge University Press.

Van Ek, J. (1986) *Objectives for Foreign Language Learning*, vol. 1: *Scope*, Strasbourg: Council of Europe.

Vygotsky, L. S. (1962) *Thought and Language*. Cambridge, Mass.: MIT Press.

Welford, A. T. (1976) *Skilled Performance: Perceptual and Motor Skills*. Glenview, Ill.: Scott, Foresman.

Widdowson, H. G. (1978) *Teaching Language as Communication.* Oxford: Oxford University Press.

Widdowson, H. G. (1979) *Explorations in Applied Linguistics.* Oxford: Oxford University Press.

Widdowson, H. G. (1990) *Aspects of Language Teaching.* Oxford: Oxford University Press.

Wilkins, D. A. (1972) *Linguistics in Language Teaching.* London: Edward Arnold.

Wilkins, D. A. (1976) *Notional Syllabuses.* Oxford: Oxford University Press.

Willis, J. (1981) *Teaching English through English.* London: Longman.

Wright, T. (1987) *The Roles of Teachers and Learners.* Oxford: Oxford University Press.

Yule, G. (1987) *The Study of Language: An Introduction.* Cambridge: Cambridge University Press.

Index